David Brandon is a
and local history wh
knows both well.

He is particularly interested in follies and the quirky and curious items which are scattered around the countryside and towns of England. A member of The Folly Fellowship, he has lectured extensively on follies and curiosities and an associated theme, English eccentricities.

His publications include several on local history and the history of crime. He is currently researching for a book on transportation to Australia (The National Archive – Public Record Office) and one on the sites of London's gallows, *The Executioners' City*.

Frontispiece
Jeffrey Hudson's birthplace (see No 17).

HUDSON'S COTTAGE

Jeffery
Hudson

SMALLEST MAN
FROM THE
SMALLEST COUNTY
IN ENGLAND

1619 - 1682

OAKHAM TOWN COUNCIL

RUTLAND
& Stamford
CURIOSITIES

David Brandon

THE DOVECOTE PRESS

ERRATUM

No 18: The Church in the Lake. The Church of St Matthew, Normanton, was only saved following a sustained campaign by the Normanton Tower Trust, founded by local people, and the author would like to apologize for any suggestion that it owes its preservation to the local authority.

No 26: The Forgotten Horsepond. The pond is known locally as the Cartwash.

No 33: Shades of the Poor Law. The building is no longer a hospital, but is used as day house accommodation by Oakham School.

First published in 2004 by The Dovecote Press Ltd
Stanbridge, Wimborne, Dorset BH21 4JD

ISBN 1 904349 25 0

Typeset in Monotype Sabon
Printed and bound by KHL Printing, Singapore

All papers used by The Dovecote Press are natural, recyclable products made from wood grown in sustainable, well-managed forests.

A CIP catalogue record for this book is available from the British Library

1 3 5 7 9 8 6 4 2

CONTENTS

1. Mystery Maze
2. Scene of Tom Cribb's Triumph
3. A Holy Well
4. Vagrancy Sign
5. A Sheela-na-gig
6. Topiary Delights
7. The Summerhouse built as a Fort
8. Where Butter was sold
9. Birthplace of a Serial Liar
10. Burial Place of Daniel Lambert
11. The Castle with Horseshoes
12. Bishop's Palace in a Village
13. Whipping Post and Stocks
14. The Model Railway Signal Box
15. 'Ram Jam Inn' Sign
16. The 'Jackson-Stops' Inn Sign
17. Birthplace of the Rutland Dwarf
18. The Church in the Lake
19. A Monumental Railway Viaduct
20. Did the Gunpowder Plot start here?
21. The Mason's Book of Samples
22. A Lost Village
23. Collegiate Gothic
24. A Norman Tour-de-force
25. A Forgotten Canal Wharf
26. The Forgotten Horsepond
27. Gothic Cemetery Chapels
28. The Horseshoe Door
29. A Fatal Epic
30. Gallows Inn Sign
31. Hunting Lodge or Dower House?
32. Memories of Sir Isaac Newton
33. Shades of the Poor Law
34. The Tools of the Stonemason

35. A Pigeon's Paradise
36. A Simple Country Church
37. Gazebo or Watch-Tower?
38. 'Tudor' Railway Station
39. A Skirmish in the Wars of the Roses
40. Shakespeare in the Garden
41. Burial Place of an Educational Pioneer
42. 'The Hurdler' Pub Sign
43. Monastic Remains in a Field
44. Health-giving Waters
45. Gateway to Education
46. The Egyptian House
47. The Burghley House Ha-ha
48. Tudor Philanthropy
49. Brewing by Steam
50. Lodges like Bottles

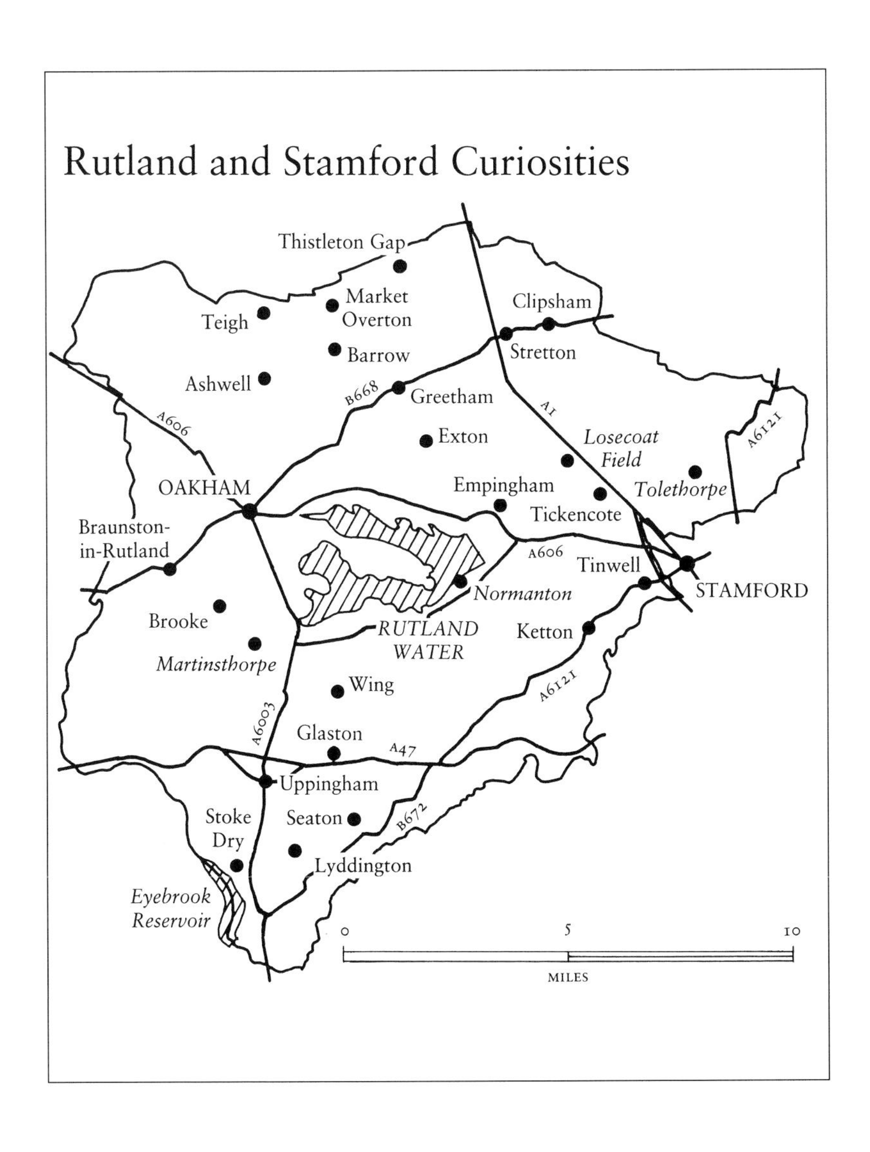
Rutland and Stamford Curiosities
Thistleton Gap
Market
Overton
Teigh
Clipsham
Barrow
Stretton
Ashwell
B668
Greetham
A606
A1
Exton
Losecoat
Field
A6121
Tolethorpe
OAKHAM
Empingham
Tickencote
Braunston-
in-Rutland
A606
Tinwell
STAMFORD
Normanton
Brooke
RUTLAND
WATER
Ketton
Martinsthorpe
Wing
A6121
A6003
Glaston
A47
Uppingham
Stoke
Dry
Seaton
B672
Lyddington
Eyebrook
Reservoir
0
5
10
MILES

INTRODUCTION

Despite its size and reputation as the smallest of all English counties, Rutland is rich in character and awash with unexpected delights. The motto of the old county of Rutland was *Multum in Parvo* and there is indeed much diversity and much to see within its boundaries. Those who were born and brought up there, and many of those who have moved in, tend to be extremely proud of the simple beauty of its landscape and its villages. However, it could be said that they keep their knowledge largely to themselves and Rutland has never been allowed to become too self-conscious or precious. By today's standards at least, Rutland is extremely peaceful and the locals like it that way. Rutland Water attracts visitors in large numbers but elsewhere and even in some of the best-known villages, there is a feeling of seclusion. There is only one substantial industrial plant.

Rutland borders four counties; Leicestershire to the west and north-west; Lincolnshire to the east and north-east; Northamptonshire to the south and Cambridgeshire to the south-east. Rutland is about 17 miles from north to south and roughly the same along its west to east axis. Much of the county is on a plateau some 400 to 500 feet above sea level. The rocks of which this area is composed, ironstone in the west and oolitic limestone in the east, have long been used for building purposes, hence the attractive use of stone in the villages and hamlets. Many of the best of the old buildings are roofed with slates from Collyweston, just across the Northamptonshire border.

This is pastoral country with traces of ancient forest in the south-west. Between Oakham and Uppingham, much of Rutland is hilly with deep descents into and climbs out of the disproportionately large valleys that the rivers Eye Brook, Chater and Gwash have cut for themselves as they flow eastwards, eventually to join the Welland. Although the creation of the reservoir which became Rutland Water was controversial, it is now generally agreed that this extremely large stretch of water enhances the attractiveness of the landscape. North of Oakham, the fertile and flatter Vale of Catmose adds further diversity. Man's long settlement in Rutland and this topographical diversity is reflected in the curiosities which can be found within its borders.

Stamford is just beyond Rutland's eastern border and probably has more in common with Rutland than it does with its own county of Lincolnshire. It is well-known for being one of England's most attractive stone-built smallish towns and its position athwart the Great North Road, as a bridging point of the River Welland and focus of several other roads, has long made it an important settlement. It was one of the five Danish boroughs, it had a castle and a market dating back to early Norman times, several monastic establishments and more than 15 parish churches. Several of Stamford's curiosities reflect the significant role that the town has long played in national affairs. Unlike Rutland in general, Stamford attracts substantial numbers of visitors. It is likely, however, that the largely unsung and understated nature of this delightful part of England means that much of its fascinating and quirky physical evidence of the past has not received the attention it deserves. If this book encourages local residents and visitors alike to eschew the more obvious attractions and take time out to develop their knowledge of history by probing into the quaint, the peculiar and the eccentric, then this author, for one, will feel he has achieved his purpose.

I would like to thank the staff at Oakham and Stamford Libraries and the staff at the Record Office for Leicestershire, Leicester and Rutland, especially Margaret Bonney, for their supportive efforts. Also the following for their moral and material support: Jane Brandon, Ed Brandon, Mark Game, Alan Brooke and Linda Brandon.

DAVID BRANDON
October 2004

1. MYSTERY MAZE

Position: Wing.
OS Map: Kettering, Corby and surrounding district, Sheet 141.
Map Ref: SK896028.
Access: Off A47 and A6003 on west side of unclassified road from Wing to Glaston. Freely available at all times.

Just outside the village of Wing a turf maze can be seen. It is circular, forty feet in diameter and its turf banks are cut to a depth of just over nine inches. Until late in the nineteenth century it was surrounded by a low earth bank. The pattern of the maze is relatively simple and unlikely to provide any difficulties for those attempting to find their way to the middle. Not the least curious aspect of the design is that it is identical to earlier mazes which were integrated into the floors of three French cathedrals, including Chartres.

Here in the depths of rural Rutland can be seen an English version both of the mazes of ancient Egypt which were described by Herodotus and the legendary labyrinth in Crete said to have been created by Daedalus, the father of Icarus, famous for being an early victim both of the sin of vanity and the human desire to fly.

One tradition says that mazes were devised by the medieval Christian Church to provide a means for public penance. Wrongdoers were placed in them and left to find their own way out, shuffling along on their hands and knees as they did so in a public show involving both humility and humiliation. Alternatively, there are those who argue that mazes were brought back to this country by Crusaders and pilgrims who had ventured into holy places in the East. They knew that the maze was an ancient motif and they may have adopted it to suggest the idea that despite the alluring temptations of sin, there was a path to Salvation, albeit a convoluted one, for those who steadfastly sought to follow the ways of Christ.

Another explanation is that many such mazes were designed for communal fun. The object of the sport was to run round them in the shortest possible time without either stumbling or touching the banks even at the sharp bends. Having reached the centre, the competitor then raced back to the start, subject to the same rules. A different sort of pleasure is suggested by those who believe that mazes were the location for pre-Christian fertility rites.

Wing maze is small compared to the eight other surviving turf mazes in England. There were once undoubtedly many more, but

The turf maze at Wing.

there is no effective way of dating them. Their mystery simple adds to their fascination.

On maps the location of mazes is often marked as 'Troy Town'. This curious name is said to derive from a game mentioned by Virgil (70-19 BC) that involved young horsemen racing while manoeuvring their way along a tortuous track or maze. Another explanation is that the walls of Troy were deliberately designed to confuse enemies, being riddled with dead-end passages, thereby creating the prototype maze. It was a widely held belief in medieval and Tudor England that the English were descended from the Trojans.

Places of Interest in the Neighbourhood

18. The Church in the Lake (Rutland Water)
22. A Lost Village (Martinsthorpe)
26. The Forgotten Horsepond (Glaston)

2. THE SCENE OF TOM CRIBB'S TRIUMPH

Position: Thistleton Gap.
OS Map: Grantham and surrounding district, Sheet 130.
Map Ref: SK904183
Access: On unclassified road from Thistleton to Sewstern. The scene of the fight is cultivated countryside visible from road. No particular landmark.

Pugilism was a sport that very much cut across class lines. Those who followed the sport extended from the humblest labourers to the most plutocratic of landed grandees. Spectators and gamblers from opposite poles of the social spectrum could be found attending the same bouts. In the early seventeenth century there were few rules and contestants not only belaboured each other with their bare fists but used wrestling holds and head-butted their opponents. Serious injuries and death could ensue.

Gradually a number of rules were brought in which allowed the sport to be based a little more on skill than simply on brute strength and ferocity. Highly skilled boxers like Daniel Mendoza and 'Gentleman' Jackson even opened boxing schools and were courted by a sporting aristocracy happy to bask in the reflected glory of having associates who were champion pugilists. Several thousand spectators would turn out to watch the best-known fighters but the sport became increasingly disreputable and it was made illegal in the

Tom Cribb fighting Molyneux at Thistleton Gap in 1811.

mid-1830s. It was only as late as 1867 that boxing was regularised and the Queensbury Rules were introduced.

In many places the magistrates moved to prevent public contests on the grounds that they attracted large, unruly, and often drunken crowds and threatened a breach of the peace. For this reason even before the 1830s, fights were often staged in remote places where the forces of law and order were thin on the ground or, as is the case with Thistleton, where county boundaries were close by and contestants and crowds could slip over the border, in this case into Lincolnshire or Leicestershire where they were immune from the magistrates of Rutland. In 1811 close by at Thistleton Gap, in a spot called 'No Man's Land', there was a fight between Tom Cribb, champion of All-England and his challenger, Tom Molyneux, a black American who claimed to be the heavyweight champion of the world. Tom Cribb won the contest with ease.

It is interesting to note that athletes in those days were considerably less rigorous in the dietary regime to which they subjected themselves. Just a few minutes before the bout was due to begin, Cribb fortified himself with a roast chicken, a large apple pie and several pints of porter.

Near to Thistleton Gap is a farm called 'Cribb's Lodge'. The Ram Jam Inn not far away at Stretton on the Great North Road for many years had a 'Tom Cribb Room'. Legend has it that the night before the fight, Cribb stayed at the Black Bull Inn at North Witham, just over the border in Lincolnshire and Molyneux slept at what was then called the New Inn at Greetham.

Places of Interest in the Neighbourhood

3. A Holy Well (Ashwell)
4. Vagrancy Sign (Barrow)
13. Whipping Posts and Stocks (Market Overton)
15. 'Ram Jam Inn' Sign (Stretton)
16. 'Jackson-Stops' Inn Sign (Stretton)
23. Collegiate Gothic (Teigh)
25. A Forgotten Canal Wharf (Market Overton)
32. Memories of Sir Isaac Newton (Market Overton)

3. A HOLY WELL

Position: Ashwell.
OS Map: Grantham and surrounding area, Sheet 130.
Map Ref: SK864136.
Access: At the junction of unclassified roads from Oakham to Wymondham and Ashwell to Langham. Easily accessible in a copse by the side of the road.

Wells and springs have long been regarded as special, sacred places. In pre-Christian times the deities who were believed to provide the precious gift of water needed to be propitiated and therefore offerings and sacrifices were made in the hope of ensuring a regular supply.

By trial and error it was established that many wells exuded water that had therapeutic qualities, the result, it was thought, of the beneficence of the gods who guarded them. The Christian Church disliked the enthusiasm of the native population for the worshipping of pagan water gods, many of whom remained loyal to their traditional beliefs even after converting to Christianity. The Church pragmatically, or even cynically it could be said, rededicated large numbers of holy wells to various Christian saints but especially to Saints Agnes, Anne and Helen. The well was then promoted on the basis of its curative powers and used to provide a valuable source of revenue for a local church or monastery. Not all wells were commercially exploited in this way. Some, still regarded as having mysterious powers for good, were what we would now describe as wishing wells.

No evidence exists that the Holy Well at Ashwell became the object of pilgrimage by those from afar. Indeed its existence perhaps would only have been known to those living in the vicinity but superstition may have led to its use as a wishing well. This well has a stone surround surmounted by a small cross and a rather battered stone panel inscribed:

All ye who hither come to drink,
Rest not your thoughts below,
Look at that sacred sign and think,
Whence living waters flow.

Close to the south door of the parish church of St Mary at Ashwell is the grave of the Rev. James Williams Adams, once rector of

The Holy Well, Ashwell.

Ashwell and the first clergyman to receive the Victoria Cross. He was reputed at one time to be the strongest man in Ireland. He served as a chaplain in India and in the Afghan wars, and died in 1903, having been in the parish for only about a year.

Places of Interest in the Neighbourhood:

4. Vagrancy Sign (Barrow)
13. Whipping Post and Stocks (Market Overton)
23. Collegiate Gothic (Teigh)
25. A Forgotten Canal Wharf (Market Overton)
32. Memories of Sir Isaac Newton (Market Overton)

4. VAGRANCY SIGN

Position: Barrow.
OS Map: Grantham and surrounding area, Sheet 130.
Map Ref: SK891151.
Access: In the hamlet of Barrow off the unclassified road from Cottesmore to Teigh. Easily visible from the road on the side of a house but located on private property.

At the east end of the small settlement of Barrow there is a curious wooden sign on the wall of an ancient thatched cottage. The sign reads as follows:

> All Vagrants who are found Beg
> ging in this Town will be taken up &
> PROSECUTED.

Vagrancy has always been frowned upon by the authorities, not least because vagrants were seen as undesirable characters with criminal tendencies or likely to incite social unrest. They were also visible, embarrassing and irritating evidence of the failure of the economic and social policies of the time.

In medieval society the responsibility of caring for the infirm, the needy and the otherwise disadvantaged was seen as a Christian duty and was carried out partly by the parish and partly by the monasteries. Much support was also raised within families and local communities for those incapable of supporting themselves.

A crucial distinction was made in the fourteenth century between those described as 'sturdy beggars' and the 'needy' or 'impotent' poor. The implication was that 'sturdy beggars' were those capable of work but who wilfully avoided working for a living. The authorities believed that they should be forced to seek gainful employment and be stigmatised if they refused. The 'needy' however were the victims of genuine misfortune who could not support themselves fully. This rough-and-ready distinction has continued to bedevil social policy to this day but it became a major issue after the Dissolution of the Monasteries in the sixteenth century. Legislation passed during the reign of Elizabeth I introduced the concept of each parish being responsible for the care of its own needy folk, who were paid for by a tax or poor rate levied on local owners of property.

Communities across the country gradually became embroiled in wider economic changes which required mobility of labour.

Substantial numbers of men began tramping to and fro in search of work while at the same time threatening bands of 'sturdy vagabonds' inhabited the thickets and highways preying on travellers. For these reasons parishes did all they could to deter strangers who might be robbers, or who might seek to settle within their boundaries and possibly become a charge on the local ratepayers.

This may be the historical background to the odd sign at Barrow intended to deter vagrants by threatening them with prosecution. In practice this usually meant that those found guilty would be whipped. However, it is unlikely that this sign is actually in situ. Although Barrow at one time was probably a settlement of some substance, and indeed the truncated remains of a cross stand close by, no one would ever describe it as a 'town'. The sign may therefore have been brought in from elsewhere. It is still a significant historical curiosity.

Like highwaymen, poachers were frequently regarded as heroes, probably because they filled their larders with game belonging to the rich and privileged. A former resident of Barrow was one Jack Thompson of whom it was proudly said that he did not need snares or traps but could take a hare with his bare hands.

Places of Interest in the Neighbourhood

3. A Holy Well (Ashwell)
13. Whipping Post and Stocks (Market Overton)
23. Collegiate Gothic (Teigh)
25. A Forgotten Canal Wharf (Market Overton)
32. Memories of Sir Isaac Newton (Market Overton)

5. SHEELA-NA-GIG

Position: Braunston-in-Rutland.
OS Map: Kettering, Corby and surrounding area, Sheet 141.
Map Ref: SK832066.
Access: Off an unclassified road from Oakham to Tilton-on-the-Hill. In the churchyard in the centre of the village and against the outside wall of the west end of the church. Freely accessible at all reasonable times.

Braunston is typical of Rutland in being an unsung and largely unvisited village, in this case composed mainly of limestone and ironstone houses of varying vintage and style. To explore in a leisurely way its higgledy-piggledy back lanes and greens is to enjoy the delights that only rural England can offer.

Against the south wall of the tower of the parish church of All Saints stands a strange crudely-carved stone figure of unknown date, origin and purpose. It is about four feet high and the upper part is carved with what appear to be grotesquely protruding eyes, a huge mouth and breasts. The figure's obvious sexual connotations must at one time have aroused disapproval from those with censorious instincts because for many years it was turned upside down and used as a doorstep. It was rediscovered early in the twentieth century during restoration work and put back on view.

This figure has been categorised by some archaeologists as a sheela-na-gig, and probably dates to between 600 and the end of the twelfth century. Carvings of this sort are not common, the best-known one probably being that at Kilpeck in Herefordshire. They are thought originally to have been pagan fertility symbols and indeed in some of them the sexual aspect is considerably more explicit.

Another explanation of the purpose of such figures is that they were a silent sermon in stone reminding the observer of the fifth of the Seven Deadly Sins – lechery.

The curious name is said to derive from an Irish phrase meaning 'Sheila of the Paps', suitably bowdlerised by the Victorians into a euphemism which it was hoped would frustrate the prurient.

Places of Interest in the Neighbourhood

8. Butter Cross (Oakham)
9. Birthplace of a Serial Liar (Oakham)
11. Castle with Horsehoes (Oakham)

The sheela-na-gig, Braunston-in-Rutland.

14. The Model Railway Signal Box (Oakham)
17. Birthplace of the Rutland Dwarf (Oakham)
22. A Lost Village (Martinsthorpe)
27. Gothic Cemetery Chapels (Oakham)
33. Shades of the Poor Law (Oakham)
36. A Simple Country Church (Brooke)

6. TOPIARY DELIGHTS

Position: Clipsham.
OS Map: Grantham and surrounding Area, Sheet 130.
Map Ref: SK979168.
Access: North-east of Clipsham on the unclassified road to Little Bytham. Open at all reasonable times.

On the north side of the by-road from Clipsham to Little Bytham can be seen a glorious extravaganza of topiary. Bordering what was once the carriage drive to Clipsham Hall are about 150 yew trees which have been cut into the shape of sugar loaves topped with birds, fishes and a wide range of other fanciful designs, some easily recognisable, others less so. Many of them also display inscriptions and other motifs in relief. This work was started in 1870 by Amos Alexander, one of the employees of the Clipsham estate, and has been carried on by others so that what can be seen is a living collection of topiary, admirably being added to or altered to reflect new ideas and contemporary events as they occur.

Places of Interest in the Neighbourhood:
15. 'Ram Jam Inn' Sign (Stretton)
16. 'Jackson-Stops' Inn Sign (Stretton)
21. A Mason's Book of Samples (Greetham)
39. A Skirmish in the Wars of the Roses (Losecoat Field)

Topiary at Clipsham Hall.

7. THE SUMMERHOUSE BUILT AS A FORT

Position: Exton Park Estate.
OS Map: Grantham and surrounding area, Sheet 130.
Map Ref: SK917114.
Access: Exton Park Estate is off the B668 from Oakham to Stretton. By public footpath from Exton Village. Although there is no public access to Fort Henry itself, there is a public footpath along the opposite side of the lake from which the building may be easily viewed.

The park at Exton was laid out around 1640. In the middle of the eighteenth century, the Noel family enlarged the park aping the so-called 'natural' style of Lancelot 'Capability' Brown and, not surprisingly, constructed a large lake. Standing by this lake is a neo-Gothick summerhouse or some think a fishing pavilion first known, appropriately, as Pond House and then later as Fort Henry. It was built by Henry, 6th Earl of Gainsborough, and it is said that he used to re-enact great sea battles on the lake, with servants from the estate acting as the crew of miniature men-of-war.

This folly is hard to date but is thought to have been built after 1785 and before 1815. It is stuccoed, has mock castellations, openwork pinnacles and a mixture of quatrefoil and ogee-headed windows. It was once topped by a dome. Underneath there is a boathouse. An excellent view of Fort Henry can be had from the opposite side of the lake.

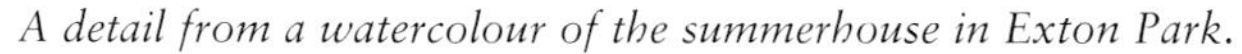
A detail from a watercolour of the summerhouse in Exton Park.

Fort Henry is only one among a number of follies in Exton Park. Until the 1990s, just to its west, there stood the Bark Temple. This was perhaps the finest English example of a fashionable but short-lived landscape conceit. It was a mock temple, in a vaguely Moorish style, composed entirely of timber and bark, nailed together and designed initially as a bandstand to provide the music for revelries by the lake and in the summerhouse. Obviously it was a fragile structure and it was allowed to deteriorate to the extent that it eventually collapsed. It may have now been restored but there is no public access.

Close to the present Exton Hall and visible from the churchyard of St Peter and St Paul is an unusual octagonal mid eighteenth century combined byre and dovecote, built at a time when dovecotes were going out of fashion. It is probable that this whimsical structure, as well as having a practical purpose, was designed to be an eye-catcher from the old Exton Hall which was burned down in 1810.

Exton Park is now largely given over to farmland and is private. The footpaths that cross it are well marked and walkers are strongly advised to keep to these at all times.

On no account should the church of St Peter and St Paul be omitted by visitors to the Exton area. That formidable art historian, Sir Nikolaus Pevsner in *The Buildings of England, Leicestershire and Rutland*, states, 'There are few churches in Rutland and few in England in which English sculpture from the 16th century to the 18th century can be studied so profitably and enjoyed so much as at Exton.' The monuments concerned trace the evolving history of the Noel and Harrington families and date from around 1380 to 1766, and include works by sculptors of the calibre of Grinling Gibbons and Joseph Nollekens.

Places of Interest in the Neighbourhood

15. 'Ram Jam Inn' Sign (Stretton)
16. 'Jackson-Stops' Inn Sign (Stretton)
21. A Mason's Book of Samples (Greetham)
24. A Norman Tour-de- force (Tickencote)
35. A Pigeon's Paradise (Empingham)
39. A Skirmish in the Wars of the Roses (Losecoat Field)

8. WHERE BUTTER WAS SOLD

Position: Oakham.
OS Map: Kettering, Corby and surrounding area, Sheet 141.
Map Ref: SK861088.
Access: Close to the Market Place in Oakham town centre. Freely available at all times.

In a corner of Oakham's attractive, L-shaped market place close to Oakham School can be seen the former Butter Cross. This is polygonal and built around a sturdy stone pillar, has a pyramidal roof of Colleyweston slates and was put up in the seventeenth century on the site of an ancient market cross. It is topped by an ancient sundial.

Until the concentration of population into the towns associated with the Industrial Revolution and the development of cheap and easy forms of transport, fairs and markets were important places for trading. The system of granting charters for the provision of markets was regularised by the Crown after the Norman Conquest. In the

Oakham Butter Cross.

thirteenth century, for example, no fewer than 3,300 charters were granted. This practice provided useful income for the Crown, enabled local landowners to enjoy the revenue from market tolls and also brought prosperity to the tradesmen and to the communities where the markets were situated.

Such crosses may have been intended to sanctify commercial transactions or to commemorate the granting of the market's charter. They were evidence of the status of the community concerned and also provided a focal point from which traders, those attending market and others could be addressed by local officials and perhaps also itinerant preachers. The cross also made a convenient point at which tolls payable for trading on the market could be collected. Most of these crosses are medieval in origin but sometimes in especially prosperous communities, they were refashioned in late medieval and Tudor times and the work was paid for by a local benefactor. Such crosses were frequently polygonal and open-sided with roofs often topped with a lantern or a cross. Oakham's cross is thought to date from the sixteenth century.

Under the shelter of the Butter Cross stands a curious set of stocks with five holes for the legs of the local ne'er-do-wells. It is tempting to think that one of Oakham's reprobates in ancient times had only one leg and two mates with the normal complement. The three of them were constantly falling foul of the authorities who eventually paid the one-legged rascal an indirect complement by designing new stocks with him specifically in mind! More likely, however, is the mundane explanation that the stocks originally had six holes but lost one of them through rot or other damage. Whippings also took place under the cross until 1765.

Places of Interest in the Neighbourhood:

9. Birthplace of a Serial Liar (Oakham)
11. The Castle with Horseshoes (Oakham)
14. The Model Railway Signal Box (Oakham)
17. Birthplace of the Rutland Dwarf (Oakham)
27. Gothic Cemetery Chapels (Oakham)
33. Shades of the Poor Law (Oakham)

9. BIRTHPLACE OF A SERIAL LIAR

Position: Oakham.
OS MAP: Kettering, Corby and surrounding Area, Sheet 141.
Map Ref: SK859089.
Access: In the town centre. The Market Place is freely open to pedestrians at all times.

In 1649 in a house in the Market Place, long since demolished, was born a baby boy who was christened Titus Oates. It would be hard in searching the annals of British history to find a less likeable character than Oates. Even as a youth he excelled in the negative qualities of dishonesty and duplicity.

Oates lived through a period when England was in the throes of mass hysteria around the perceived threat of a Catholic conspiracy to regain Catholicism's dominance in the Christian world. Oates was ordained into the Church of England, by which time he had developed a great hatred of Catholicism, and in 1677 he became a Catholic himself in order to gain a better understanding of his enemy. With an equally unsavoury associate, Oates concocted the simple but fiendish 'Popish Plot' to assassinate Charles II and place the country under the control of the Jesuits.

Oates related with relish how the plotters, whose base was a London tavern, had boasted that the gutters would soon be running with Protestant blood. This information was passed on to a zealous magistrate, Sir Edmund Berry Godfrey. When he was found dead on Hampstead Heath run through with his own sword a few days later, many people concluded that this was evidence that the Popish Plot had started and that the English way of life was under imminent threat.

Oates now found himself being willingly propelled into the forefront of affairs. He pointed the finger at one Edward Coleman who he accused of bribing assassins to kill the King. On concocted evidence and false testimony, Coleman was tried and executed at Tyburn. Oates was the hero of the moment. Between the end of 1678 and the beginning of 1681 about thirty-five people were tried, convicted and executed for their part in a completely imaginary plot. The convictions were made on the basis of false information and perjured statements made by Oates and his associates.

Oates, however, overstepped the mark when he accused Charles II's wife, Catherine of Braganza, of being involved in the plot. No one believed him and his fall from grace was rapid. He was convicted of perjury, unfrocked, imprisoned and heavily fined as well as being placed in the pillory with a paper on his head listing his crimes. Such was the disgust of the London crowd with his behaviour that they pelted him enthusiastically with dead cats, dogs and rats – nearly killing him in the process. He was released from prison after James II was deposed, later resurfacing as a Baptist minister. He was, however, dismissed because of what were euphemistically described as 'financial irregularities'. He died in 1705, by which time his name had become synonymous with systematic falsehoods.

The great Victorian historian, Thomas Macaulay has provided a wonderful description of Oates: 'his short neck, his legs uneven, the vulgar said, as those of a badger, his forehead low as that of a baboon, his purple cheeks, and his monstrous length of chin, had all been familiar to those who frequented the courts of law . . . Times had now changed, and many who had formerly regarded him as the deliverer of the country, shuddered at the sight of those hideous features on which villainy seemed to be written by the hand of God'.

Places of Interest in the Neighbourhood

8. Where Butter was sold (Oakham)
11. The Castle with Horseshoes (Oakham)
14. The Model Railway Signal Box (Oakham)
17. Birthplace of the Rutland Dwarf (Oakham)
27. Gothic Cemetery Chapels (Oakham)
33. Shades of the Poor Law (Oakham)

10. BURIAL PLACE OF DANIEL LAMBERT

Position: Stamford.
OS Map: Kettering, Corby and surrounding area, Sheet 141.
Map Ref: TF31068.
Access: The headstone is in the detached burial ground which stands a short distance from the church of St Martin's Without in Stamford. Off A43 and B1443. Freely accessible at all times.

Daniel Lambert was born in Leicester in 1770 and enjoyed normal health until the age of 20. He was an athletic youth with a considerable love for outdoor sports but he then developed a medical condition which caused him to gain weight so rapidly that by the age of 23 he weighed 32 stone.

He was forced to give up his job as a gaoler in the Leicester House of Correction either because of his physical condition, or, according to other accounts, because the gaol closed. He had certainly started putting on weight by this time and was strong enough, so legend says, to have used a stout stick to see off a performing bear which had attacked a dog in the street. He was by nature rather shy and although he had a small pension, he had little option but to make an income by exhibiting himself to a public always agog to view human peculiarities. He had a ready wit and was popular with those who flocked to see him at the various addresses in London he took as lodgings. He also made tours of the provinces, bearing himself with great dignity and good humour, and charging the then considerable sum of one shilling for entry to his presence.

In 1809 he came to Stamford apparently on his way to or from Huntingdon races or possibly the races which used to be held just outside Stamford itself. He had now achieved the astounding weight of 52 stone 11 pounds and a girth of 112 inches. He lodged at the now defunct Waggon and Horses Inn where he was found dead one morning.

To remove his corpse for burial part of the building had to be demolished. Lambert's coffin was six feet four inches long, four feet four inches wide and two feet four inches deep. It was moved to the churchyard on wheels. When the perspiring coffin bearers arrived at the graveside, they realised, despite the fact that there were at least 20 of them, that it was impossible to lower the coffin into the grave in the normal way so a ramp was hastily dug to enable them to step down with the coffin into the extremely large hole that had been excavated to provide Lambert's last resting place.

Nearby, the famous George Inn displays the necessarily stout walking stick of this gentle, likeable but tragic man. The Stamford Museum in Broad Street contains a life-size model of Lambert in some of his original clothes. His excessive weight was nothing to do with his dietary habits because he ate little and eschewed alcohol but today doctors would probably ascribe it to metabolic problems or perhaps a disorder of the endocrine glands.

The words that appear on his headstone are:

In Remembrance of that PRODIGY in NATURE
DANIEL LAMBERT a Native of LEICESTER
who was possessed of an exalted and convivial Mind
and, in personal Greatness had no COMPETITOR:
He measured three feet one Inch round the LEG
Nine Feet four Inches round the Body
And weighed FIFTY TWO STONE ELEVEN POUNDS
He departed this Life on the 21st of June 1809
AGED 39 YEARS

As a Testimony of Respect this Stone
is erected by his Friends in Leicester

Places of Interest in the Neighbourhood

30. Gallows Inn Sign (Stamford)
31. Hunting Lodge or Dower House? (Wothorpe)
38. 'Tudor' Railway Station (Stamford)
42. 'The Hurdler' Pub Sign (Stamford)
43. St Leonard's Priory (Stamford)
44. Health-giving Waters (Stamford)
45. Gateway to Education (Stamford)
46. The Egyptian House (Stamford)
47. The Burghley House Ha-ha (Burghley Park)
48. Tudor Philanthropy (Stamford)
49. Brewing by Steam (Stamford)
50. Lodges like Bottles (Burghley Park)

Daniel Lambert

11. THE CASTLE WITH HORSESHOES

Position: Oakham.
OS Map: Kettering, Corby and surrounding area, Sheet 141.
Map Ref: SK861088.
Access: In a public park close to the Market Place. The building itself is used as a courtroom but is open for visitors at other times.

One of the best-known sights of Rutland is Oakham Castle, a remnant of a late twelfth century castle of some substance. Its origins probably lay with a motte and bailey structure. The later curtain walls and other buildings have largely disappeared. To the north in what is now a public park are some slight traces of the castle's fishponds and gardens. What can be seen now is the great hall, which is the earliest and the best preserved of its kind in England. It is constructed of ironstone rubble with ashlar dressings and was once in the hands of the powerful Ferrers family.

The Great Hall, Oakham Castle.

What probably draws most visitors to Oakham Castle, however, is the curious and unique collection of horseshoes, numbering well over 200, with which the great hall, which doubles as a magistrates' court, is decorated. It is believed that in the fifteenth century, or perhaps before, a tradition developed whereby the local lord of the manor was entitled to demand a toll of a token horseshoe from any peer or member of royalty who was passing through the town. The collection was started with an outsize shoe given by Edward IV in about 1470 and has continued to this day. The name of the presenter is inscribed on each shoe and where appropriate the shoes are topped with coronets. Some are small and rusty, others large and well-gilded. Now that the horseshoe has been adopted as the county's emblem, the collection is particularly appropriate.

In 1843 a small shoe presented to the collection by Lord Willoughby d'Eresby was stolen by boys from Oakham School. It was eventually returned by a country clergyman on behalf of the boys who were desperate to get rid of it because of the various misfortunes that had befallen each of them while it was in their possession.

Places of Interest in the Neighbourhood

8. Where Butter was sold (Oakham)
9. Birthplace of a Serial Liar (Oakham)
14. The Model Railway Signal Box (Oakham)
17. Birthplace of the Rutland Dwarf (Oakham)
27. Gothic Cemetery Chapels (Oakham)
33. Shades of the Poor Law (Oakham)

12. THE BISHOP'S PALACE IN A VILLAGE

Position: Lyddington.
OS Map: Kettering, Corby and surrounding area, Sheet 141.
Map Ref: SK878970.
Access: In the centre of the village off A6003. The Bede House is in the care of English Heritage. Enquire for opening times.

This seemly village of limestone and rich reddy-brown ironstone houses is 2 miles south of Uppingham close to the Welland Valley. It preserves many delights including the so-called Bede House.

In 1085, when the diocese of Lincoln was being established, William I gave the bishop a large estate in this part of Rutland. In the reign of King John (1199-1216), a palace was built at Lyddington to house the bishop in some splendour when he was making a progress around his vast diocese, which at that time stretched from the Humber to the Thames.

The present building, however, dates from the late fifteenth and early sixteenth centuries and very much retains the appearance of a medieval episcopal palace, with an especially fine banqueting hall displaying a superb oak panelled ceiling. Heraldic glass from these early times can still be seen in the mullioned windows and the building also contains fine staircases. The Bishops of Lincoln were immensely rich and powerful but even they were no match for the rapacious Henry VIII who forced them to surrender the palace in 1547.

It was then bought by the Cromwell family and sold on later to the Cecils of Burghley House near Stamford. Thomas Cecil, son of Lord Burghley, Queen Elizabeth's wily but staunch chief minister, converted it into almshouses at which time it was known as 'Jesus Hospital'. The inmates were poor or 'impotent' men and women who in return for receiving charity were required to pray for the souls of their benefactors. The residential function of the Lyddington Bede House has ceased but the income from the original endowment now goes to out-pensioners who are nominated for this benefit by the descendents of Thomas Cecil. The title of the Cecils lives on in the village where one of the pubs is called the Marquess of Exeter.

The Bede House is probably unique in this country for being at one and the same time a medieval palace and a seventeenth century almshouse.

The Bede House, Lyddington.

Places of Interest in the Neighbourhood

19. A Monumental Railway Viaduct (Seaton)
20. Did the Gunpowder Plot start here? (Stoke Dry)
29. A Fatal Epic (Uppingham)
37. Gazebo or Watch-tower? (Lyddington)
41. Burial Place of an Educational Pioneer (Uppingham)

13. WHIPPING POST AND STOCKS

Position: Market Overton.
OS Map: Grantham and surrounding area, Sheet 130.
Map Ref: SK887163.
Access: In the centre of Market Overton on unclassified roads off the B668. Freely available at all times.

On the green at Market Overton can be seen the old village stocks and whipping post. These are relics from a past age in which local communities were much more self-contained than they are today and when petty offenders, probably known to all the villagers, needed to be punished and deterred from further wrong-doing.

What could be better than a punishment which everyone could see and which involved public humiliation and ridicule? Locked into the stocks which were usually located at some central point in the village, the offender was then made the butt of verbal derision and, frequently, of missiles such as stones but also rotting vegetables and other noisome material. The victim was totally incapable of retaliation or even of defending himself. Old enemies came to gloat at his discomfiture and whatever standing he may have previously had in the community was effectively reduced to nought. The stocks at Market Overton were last used in 1838.

The types of offence for which this punishment was levied included stealing wood, cheating at cards, frequenting the alehouse during divine service, drunkenness, blasphemy and various minor sexual peccadilloes. Vagrants also frequently found themselves sitting in the stocks ruminating woefully on their fecklessness. Affront to dignity and injury from hard missiles apart, a spell in the stocks could also be exquisitely painful. Offenders could not scratch themselves, they might get excruciating cramps, they could become thirsty and hungry and were unable to relieve themselves without further humiliation.

Whipping was usually administered for offences of a rather more serious nature. Being so easy to administer, it almost became a judicial panacea for a wide range of offences. Again, humiliation in front of one's peers was crucial and the more visible infliction of pain usually drew substantial numbers of spectators.

There is a local legend that the joiner who made these stocks, one John Wilbourne, was among the first people to be placed in them although the nature of his offence is not specified.

The village stocks, Market Overton.

Places of Interest in the Neighbourhood

2. Scene of Tom Cribb's Triumph (Thistleton Gap)
4. Vagrancy Sign (Barrow)
23. Collegiate Gothic (Teigh)
25. A Forgotten Canal Wharf (Market Overton)
32. Memories of Sir Isaac Newton (Market Overton)

14. THE MODEL RAILWAY SIGNAL BOX

Position: Just west of Oakham town centre.
OS Map: Kettering, Corby and surrounding area, Sheet 141.
Map Ref: SK857089.
Access: On A606. Readily visible from the road.

Back in the 1960s, Airfix bought out a series of plastic kits of locomotives and other railway equipment. One of these was a signal box. Their choice fell on this small wooden signal box called Oakham Level Crossing, turning a hitherto unsung signal box into something of a celebrity as miniature versions of this prototype appeared on 00-gauge model railways right across the land.

Oakham is an intermediate station on what was originally the Syston and Peterborough Railway. This line was opened in stages, the section through Oakham opening in 1848. The signal box, however, dates from 1899 and any railway enthusiast worth his salt would be able to tell you immediately that it is of typical Midland Railway design. The Midland Railway with its headquarters at Derby was one of the largest pre-grouping railway companies and had grown vast by absorbing smaller companies such the Syston and Peterborough.

One of the fascinating aspects of Britain's old railway companies was the way in which they developed their own distinctive 'house styles'. This could be seen not only in signal boxes but station buildings and fittings, signals, fencing and, more glamorously, in rolling stock and locomotives. Most of this equipment has of course been swept away but the line through Oakham – which now forms part of a major rail artery joining East Anglia to the Midlands and north-west has retained a number of similar mechanical signal boxes and some of the associated mechanical quadrant signals. The line is due for upgrading which will involve the replacement of outdated signalling equipment and this signal box will then become redundant. Like the main station building, it is listed, but its eventual fate as and when it goes out of use is by no means clear.

Oakham signal box controls an exceptionally busy level crossing and holds up hundreds of impatient motorists every day. How many of them spare a thought for this small piece of living railway history?

Oakham Level Crossing Signal Box.

Places of Interest in the Neighbourhood

8. Where Butter was sold (Oakham)
9. Birthplace of a Serial Liar (Oakham)
11. The Castle with Horseshoes (Oakham)
17. Birthplace of the Rutland Dwarf (Oakham)
27. Gothic Cemetery Chapels (Oakham)
33. Shades of the Poor Law (Oakham)

15. 'RAM JAM INN' SIGN

Position: Stretton.
OS Map: Grantham and surrounding area, Sheet 130.
Map Ref: SK946159.
Access: On the northbound carriageway of the A1 west of Stretton. Open during business hours.

The Ram Jam Inn is situated between Stamford and Oakham on the west or northbound side of the A1, a road described by Sir Nikolaus Pevsner nearly fifty years ago as 'Britain's permanent pandemonium No 1'.

The origins of this pub lie in a fourteenth century thatched wayside alehouse serving travellers on the Great North Road, even then one of England's major trunk roads. The nearest villages are Stretton and Greetham.

At one time it was called 'The Winchilsea Arms' and carried a sign bearing the arms of the Finch-Hatton family. No-one knows when its name changed, but the one it bears today is unique even among the marvellous farrago of diverse and quirky historical evidence which is provided by British pub signs and names.

Legend has it that the inn got its name in the days of the long-distance stage coaches. On one occasion a coach traveller, although some say it was a highwayman, stayed here for some days and ran up a considerable bill. The evening before he planned to leave without paying his bill, he took the landlord and his wife to one side. With the air of someone bestowing a great favour, he informed them that he knew of a method of drawing two different kinds of beer from the same barrel. Not surprisingly, the couple he confided in were unimpressed by this revelation. The traveller realised that the wife was more open to his blandishments, and thus was delighted the next morning when the husband rode away on business. He had little trouble in persuading the woman of the house to accompany him into the cellar. He made a hole in one side of a full barrel and then told her to 'ram' her thumb in it before too much beer was lost. Having made a hole on the other side of the barrel he then persuaded the gullible alewife to 'jam' her thumb into this hole as well. She was left, arms and hands immobilised, while he told her that he would look for some bungs for the holes. He then decamped leaving her to ruminate at her leisure over his practical joke and the unpaid bills that he left behind.

The 'Ram Jam Inn' sign.

There are other explanations for the bizarre name of this pub. One says that in 1740 an army sergeant, son of a Rutland man who had just returned from service in India, became the landlord. He proceeded to sell a previously unknown but highly potent liquor under the name of 'Ram Jam' which he said was an Indian name for a table servant. The drink proved so popular that his hostelry became known as the 'Ram Jam Inn'. The recipe was a secret which was inherited by his son under whose tutelage the inn continued to prosper. The recipe disappeared when the son died without passing the secret on. An alternative story says that the man had his life saved by a faithful Indian servant called 'Ram Jam' and so in gratitude he named the drink after him. Another explanation of the name is that it refers to the fact that the inn was always packed with customers, evidence of the good cheer and convivial atmosphere to be had within.

Places of Interest in the Neighbourhood

2. Scene of Tom Cribb's Triumph (Thistleton Gap)
6. Topiary Delights (Clipsham)
16. 'Jackson-Stops' Inn Sign (Stretton)
21. A Mason's Book of Samples (Greetham)
39. A Skirmish in the Wars of the Roses (Losecoat Field)

16. THE 'JACKSON-STOPS' INN SIGN

Position: Stretton.
OS Map: Grantham and surrounding area, Sheet 130.
Map Ref: SK949158.
Access: On an unclassified road off the east side of the A1. Visible from the road.

Stretton is an unusual village in possessing two pubs with unique names. As well as the 'Ram Jam Inn' on the Great North Road, there is 'The Jackson-Stops' in the village.

The story of how this pub came to get its name is simple. The old pub was called the 'White Horse' and some years ago it closed and was placed on the market for residential purposes. The estate agency on whose books the pub appeared was Jackson-Stops, who naturally placed one of their 'For Sale' signs on the building. It proved difficult to find a buyer and so the building stayed closed. It had the Jackson-Stops sign on it for so long that when it eventually reopened as a pub, it was decided to give it the name by which everybody had come to know it – 'The Jackson-Stops', rather than its original name.

Rutland does not have many other unusual pub names although one is the 'Horse and Panniers' at North Luffenham, usually referred to locally as the 'Nag and Bag'. Before the transport improvements of the seventeenth and eighteenth centuries, packhorses or mules had a major role to play in the movement of goods where no suitable water transport was available. They would be tethered together in a single file train sometimes consisting of as many as forty or fifty animals and these were a common sight making their slow way along the highways of the time. The condition of Britain's roads was usually bad – dustbowls in the summer and quagmires in the winter but packhorses were able to make their way rather more easily than the ponderous wagons drawn by horses or oxen.

Places of Interest in the Neighbourhood

2. Scene of Tom Cribb's Triumph (Thistleton Gap)
6. Topiary Delights (Clipsham)
15. 'Ram Jam Inn' Sign (Stretton)
21. A Mason's Book of Samples (Greetham)
39. A Skirmish in the Wars of the Roses (Losecoat Field)

17. BIRTHPLACE OF THE RUTLAND DWARF

Position: Oakham.
OS Map: Kettering, Corby and surrounding area, Sheet 141.
Map Ref: SK857089.
Access: Oakham town centre. Private property but the frontage is easily viewed from A606.

Jeffrey Hudson was born in Oakham in 1619. His father was a butcher who kept and baited bulls for George Villiers, Duke of Buckingham. Hard facts about his life are difficult to come by but a good story can be told from what is known.

When he was 9 years of age, he was presented by his father to the Duchess of Buckingham at Burley-on-the-Hill, who promptly found him employment in her household. He was described at the time as being almost 18 inches in height and perfectly formed and proportioned, albeit in miniature. Both his parents were of normal stature.

Not long afterwards Charles I and his wife passed through Rutland and at a banquet put on in their honour by the Duke and Duchess of Buckingham, Hudson was placed in a pie and presented to the royal couple who were apparently enchanted when he climbed out and made a courtly bow. Indeed Henrietta Maria is supposed to have been so pleased with his demeanour that she took him into her service. This is when Hudson's adventures really started. In 1630 he was sent to France to escort to England a highly esteemed midwife who was to assist at Henrietta Maria's forthcoming confinement. On the way back across the English Channel he was captured by Flemish pirates.

Somehow or other Hudson turned up in 1637 as a mercenary in the service of the Prince of Orange. By this time, Hudson had gained the nickname 'Strenuous Jeffrey' for his feats of arms. It seems that he went on to be a captain in a Royalist cavalry regiment in the English Civil War and that he spent much time attending to the needs of the Queen. The fact that he was in her company so much led to a great deal of salacious gossip. In 1649 Hudson was involved in a duel in Paris. When his opponent showed his contempt for his diminutive stature by turning up armed only with a water pistol, Hudson was so incensed that he shot him in the head.

Forced to flee France in the wake of the duel, he was captured at sea by the Turks who sold him as a slave. But he was certainly back

The birthplace of Jeffrey Hudson, Oakham.

in England in 1658, and he lived quietly for some years on a pension paid for in part by the Duke of Buckingham.

Hudson's exact height is uncertain. He is believed to have stopped growing at the age of seven by which time he had reached around eighteen inches in height. Hudson always had a somewhat tetchy character and although he made his fame and fortune from his diminutive stature, we can perhaps sympathise with his well-attested irritation every time that he found himself being referred to as the man who was served up in a pie. His waistcoat, breeches and stockings are in the Ashmolean Museum in Oxford. He attracted much interest from chroniclers, story tellers and painters, the latter including Sir Anthony Van Dyck.

Hudson died in 1682. A small man but larger than life.

Places of Interest in the Neighbourhood

8. Where Butter was Sold (Oakham)
9. Birthplace of a Serial Liar (Oakham)
11. The Castle with Horseshoes (Oakham)
14. The Model Railway Signal Box (Oakham)
27. Gothic Cemetery Chapels (Oakham)
33. Shades of the Poor Law (Oakham)

18. THE CHURCH IN THE LAKE

Position: Normanton.
OS Map: Kettering, Corby and surrounding area, Sheet 141.
Map Ref: SK932063.
Access: On the south shore of Rutland Water on an unclassified road from Edith Weston to Manton. The Museum's opening times are readily obtainable. The location is well signposted.

One of the oddest sights in Rutland is that of Normanton Church standing on a promontory jutting out into Rutland Water or even perhaps looking as if it is about to subside into the cold waters. Until just after the Second World War this church stood in close proximity to the grand eighteenth century Palladian mansion of Normanton Hall, demolished in 1925 after a fire.

Normanton Church is a strangely urban-looking building to find in the middle of rural Rutland, emphasised by its location on the edge of a massive reservoir. It has a tower in the Baroque style built in the late 1820s, while the nave with its apse was built nearly a century later. As a unity this building would not look amiss in a fashionable square of London's West End. Indeed it is built in a very similar style to St John's, Smith Square, Westminster which opened for worship in 1728.

When Rutland Water was constructed in 1979, the lower part of Normanton Church would have been inundated. Instead the authorities, to their credit, decided that the church should be taken out of use and it was underpinned, waterproofed and surrounded by a protective embankment. It was converted into a museum with items related to the 3,100 acre reservoir and its environs. So there it rides, close to the south bank of the largest man-made reservoir in western Europe, and those who gaze at it have to decide whether they should thank their stars for the conservationists or scoff gently at its present slightly ridiculous situation.

The village of Normanton was swept away when Sir Gilbert Heathcote enlarged his park. Then the big house must have stood in grand aristocratic isolation with commanding views over scenic Rutland. Now just the church, a curious survivor, is alone in reminding us of past aristocratic glories in this delightful countryside. Of Normanton Hall, only the stables remain and these are now used as a restaurant and conference centre.

The Church of St Matthew, Normanton

Places of Interest in the Neighbourhood

1. Mystery Maze (Wing)
22. A Lost Village (Martinsthorpe)
34. The Tools of the Stonemason (Ketton)
35. A Pigeons' Paradise (Empingham)

19. A MONUMENTAL RAILWAY VIADUCT

Position: Seaton.
OS Map: Kettering, Corby and surrounding district, Sheet 141.
Map Ref: SK983913.
Access: The viaduct stretches across the Welland Valley from Seaton in Rutland to Harringworth in Northamptonshire. It can be viewed from below on the B672 or the unclassified road from Seaton to Harringworth.

Where it passes along the southern edge of Rutland, the River Welland, flowing eastwards, has carved out a wide and shallow valley. Spanning the valley is Britain's longest brick-built viaduct. It is over three-quarters of a mile long, has 82 arches, is about 70 feet above the valley below and is largely composed of blue engineering bricks that were manufactured in a temporary brickworks near the site. This prodigious viaduct was built in 1876-8.

Welland Viaduct.

The railway line that runs over the Welland Viaduct is on the former Nottingham-Oakham-Kettering line of the old Midland Railway; originally built in the late 1870s to give Nottingham a more direct route southwards towards London while also giving access to sizeable deposits of iron ore in the Rockingham Forest area.

Costs were high because of the need for the viaduct. Since many of the trains using the line were likely to be heavy goods or mineral trains, it was decided to restrict the gradient in the area to a gentle 1 in 142, hence the two mile-long tunnels either side of the viaduct, at Glaston on the Rutland side and at Corby.

Regular passenger trains were either diverted or withdrawn in 1966. Trains of steel coil still run to Corby and the viaduct often sees the diversion of trains from the Midland Main Line several miles to the west. Passengers crossing the viaduct can have absolutely no idea of the monumental appearance that it provides when viewed from the lanes and fields below.

Places of Interest in the Neighbourhood

12. Bishop's Palace in a Village (Lyddington)
20. Did the Gunpowder Plot start here? (Stoke Dry)
26. A Forgotten Horsepond (Glaston)
29. A Fatal Epic (Uppingham)
37. Gazebo or Watch-Tower? (Lyddington)
41. Burial Place of an Educational Pioneer (Uppingham)

20. DID THE GUNPOWDER PLOT START HERE?

Position: Stoke Dry.
OS Map: Kettering, Corby and surrounding area, Sheet 141.
Map Ref: SK856968.
Access: The hamlet of Stoke Dry is on a narrow unclassified road off the west side of A6003 about 2 miles south of Uppingham. Information on where to obtain the key can be found in the porch.

Stoke Dry is a tiny hamlet in hilly country not far from Uppingham. It possesses a fascinating little church whose churchyard provides extensive views over the valley of the River Welland and the Eyebrook Reservoir.

The Church of St Andrew displays work of all periods from the Norman to the eighteenth century and possesses fine monuments to the Digby family, many generations of whom lived at Stoke Dry. It was this family that gave the world Sir Everard Digby, born in the sixteenth century a Protestant but converted to Catholicism by a Jesuit priest and after that filled with the fanatical zeal common to religious converts. He became embroiled in the Gunpowder Plot and the planning for the Catholic uprising the plotters intended to launch following the destruction of the Houses of Parliament. He was caught, tried and eventually hanged in the churchyard of St Paul's Cathedral.

According to some accounts the infamous Gunpowder Plot was hatched in the priest's room over the north porch. Another story is that an early vicar of Stoke Dry seized a witch and incarcerated her in this little room where she died of starvation. A notice in the church provides a disclaimer for this story although the myth of the room being haunted by her ghost still attracts interest. The priest's room has a pretty oriel window with mock battlements, and was probably used as a storeroom or perhaps for the holding of Sunday school classes.

Of interest in the church are crude carvings of the Norman period on the chancel arch; one of these portrays a man apparently pulling on a bell rope and is thought to be one of the earliest depictions of bell-ringing in this country. There is also a wooden rood screen, a comparative rarity for this area; carved bench ends; some wall-paintings and various Digby monuments dating from the fifteenth and sixteenth centuries. The paintings include a clearly-identified St Christopher but a much more enigmatic scene in which St Edmund

The Church of St. Andrew, Stoke Dry.

is seen, as legend says, being put to death by arrows. The archer, however, is a most peculiar figure looking rather like a Red Indian wearing a headdress.

The Eyebrook Reservoir which can be seen from the churchyard is of some interest because it was used by the famous 617 Squadron, the 'Dam Busters', for practice with the 'bouncing bomb' which was later employed with considerable success against a number of well-defended German dams.

Places of Interest in the Neighbourhood

12. Bishop's Palace in a Village (Lyddington)
19. A Monumental Railway Viaduct (Seaton)
29. A Fatal Epic (Uppingham)
37. Gazebo or Watch-Tower? (Lyddington)
41. Burial Place of an Educational Pioneer (Uppingham)

21. THE MASON'S BOOK OF SAMPLES

Position: Greetham.
OS Map: Grantham and surrounding area, Sheet 130.
Map Re: SK926144.
Access: Halliday's Workshop is in the village of Greetham at the junction of Main Street and Great Lane. It is private property but can be viewed from the street. Greetham is on the B668.

In the middle of Greetham stands what is at first glance an unremarkable stone building. Closer examination reveals fragments of church window tracery and other motifs in masonry, placed in a random fashion along a lengthy wall. Initial impressions are of some kind of architectural folly. However, this building was the workshop of Thomas Halliday (1816-1884), who was a member of a well-known and long-standing Rutland family of stonemasons. This complex of buildings constituted his workshop. Items from buildings he had restored, samples and unwanted pieces of work were placed in public view on the wall of his workshop and made an effective advertisement or trade sign.

Documentary evidence makes it clear that Halliday had ample work. We know, for example, that he was called upon to do urgent repairs to Exton church which had been seriously damaged by lightning in 1843. It is clear that he also had contracts for work on buildings such as Lyndon Hall and Walcot Hall, including perhaps landscape and garden design. Halliday's business interests extended to farming as well, and in his heyday he was undoubtedly one of the area's biggest employers.

Places of Interest in the Neighbourhood

6. Topiary Delights (Clipsham)
7. A Summerhouse built as a Fort (Exton)
15. 'Ram Jam Inn' Sign (Stretton)
16. 'Jackson-Stops' Inn Sign (Stretton)

Halliday's Workshop, Greetham.

22. A LOST VILLAGE

Position: Martinsthorpe.
OS Map: Kettering, Corby and surrounding area, Sheet 130.
Map Ref: SK867045.
Access: Martinsthorpe is off the A6006 about three miles south of Oakham and one mile west of Manton. It is on private land but there is a public bridleway which leads through the site.

There are well over 2,000 known lost village sites in England, the heaviest concentration being along the great stone belt which extends from Dorset through the Midlands into eastern Yorkshire. Rutland alone has over a dozen such sites but the most accessible is that at Martinsthorpe.

Deserted village sites are not easy to interpret to the untrained eye. Martinsthorpe stands on a ridge overlooking the valley of the little River Chater and is simple to locate because of an impressive fragment of a building which goes by the name of 'Old Hall Farm', although it is now little more than a barn and store. Nearby are a mass of humps and indentations. These are the sites of former houses and streets, whilst one square area surrounded by what may have been a moat probably indicates the location of a former manor house. Sizeable areas of ridge and furrow, evidence of ancient cultivated fields, are also visible.

It is known that Martinsthorpe existed as a settlement in 1199 and it is believed that there was a church there because a list of rectors goes back to 1258. In 1377 the settlement was substantial enough for 39 people to be paying poll tax. In 1522 the village had become deserted because the agricultural land had been turned from arable to pasture for the grazing of sheep.

In the seventeenth century Martinsthorpe House was built close by and was contained within a park with a total extent on 75 acres. This house was demolished in 1755, probably after years of decline, and Old Hall Farm may be a remnant of this house, perhaps the stables which were converted into a farmhouse. The last residents left in 1950.

The ideal time for visiting and investigating a site of this sort is the winter months when the greenery is at its most sparse. Best of all is a winter's day with a light snow covering when the low sun greatly helps to emphasise the shapes of the remaining earthworks.

Old Hall Farm, Martinsthorpe.

Places of Interest in the Neighbourhood

1. Mystery Maze (Wing)
5. A Sheela-na-Gig (Braunston)
8. Where Butter was sold (Oakham)
9. Birthplace of a Serial Liar (Oakham)
11. The Castle with Horseshoes (Oakham)
14. The Model Railway Signal Box (Oakham)
17. Birthplace of the Rutland Dwarf (Oakham)
33. Shades of the Poor Law (Oakham)
36. A Simple Country Church (Brooke)

23. COLLEGIATE GOTHIC

Position: Teigh.
OS Map: Grantham and surrounding area, Sheet 130.
Map Ref: SK865160.
Access: Off an unclassified road from Oakham to Edmondthorpe and Wymondham. Information is available on the whereabouts of the key.

Teigh (pronounced 'Tee') lies at the heart of the Vale of Catmose and is not much more than a hamlet. It is notable for its remarkable little church of Holy Trinity. With the exception of the thirteenth century tower, the church was completely rebuilt in 1782 by George Richardson on the instructions of the Reverend Earl of Harborough. The latter's devotion to church building is also well demonstrated by the fact that he commissioned Richardson's work at other churches just across the Leicestershire border, at Saxby and Stapleford.

The church is without separate chancel or aisles and possesses an interior fitted out not unlike a college chapel with pews in tiers facing each other. Perhaps the oddest feature of this engaging little building is, however, its internal west end where there are three Gothic-style arches. The two outside ones contain the Creed and the Ten Commandments while that in the centre, above the doorway into the tower, contains two reading desks and the pulpit and most oddly, a painted background section of wall with mock glazing bars with blue sky and trees appearing behind them. Is this the only church in England in which all the members of the congregation have to turn to the west to hear the lessons and the sermon?

At the east end of the church there is a brass plaque which commemorates the fact that Teigh was one of only 31 'Thankful Villages' in Britain: the handful of villages that suffered no casualties throughout the First World War.

In the churchyard is buried Anthony Jenkinson, pioneer explorer and trader, who travelled extensively throughout Central Asia, was received by Ivan the Terrible at his court and who after many adventures, died in this sequestered part of England in 1611.

Teigh may be tranquil today, but in 1326 it witnessed a scene of extraordinary barbarity. The local de Foleville family terrorised the neighbourhood, robbing, murdering and laying waste. A force was sent to seize the leader, Richard de Foleville, and bring him to justice. He, incidentally, combined the role of priest with that of robber. He fought his would-be captors like a wildcat, killing one of them and

The Church of Holy Trinity, Teigh.

seriously wounding others. He was so hopelessly outnumbered he barricaded himself in the church. He was eventually dragged out, only to be peremptorily decapitated in his own churchyard.

Places of Interest in the Neighbourhood

1. Scene of Tom Cribb's Triumph (Thistleton Gap)
2. A Holy Well (Ashwell)
3. Vagrancy Sign (Barrow)
13. Whipping Post and Stocks (Market Overton)
25. A Forgotten Canal Wharf (Market Overton)
32. Memories of Sir Isaac Newton (Market Overton)

The chancel arch, St Peter's, Tickencote.

24. A NORMAN TOUR-DE-FORCE

Position: Tickencote.
OS Map: Kettering, Corby and surrounding area, Sheet 141.
Map Ref: SK990095.
Access: Tickencote is off the B108 close to its junction with the A1. Information on the availability of the key is posted in the porch.

Tickencote is an isolated little settlement, and remarkably quiet given its proximity to the Great North Road. It is famous for the extraordinary chancel arch in the church of St Peter. This is of six orders, all richly carved and each order is carved differently. The outermost has foliage patterns and billet moulding, the second chevron, the third foliage and grotesques, the latter potent evidence of the extent of the medieval imagination, the fourth crenellated mouldings, the fifth beak-head and the sixth and lowest has cable or rope motifs.

The arch, which must have absolutely overwhelmed the original small building – consisting of just two simple cells, a nave and chancel – is powerful but barbaric and crude. The chancel is also Norman, with an extremely unusual six-part stone-ribbed vault with a fine central boss. This shows a monk's head and two muzzled bears and is a rare example of a surviving Norman roof boss.

The font is thirteenth-century. It is square, has dog-tooth ornament and decorative interlaced arches. In 1236, the then Archbishop of Canterbury, concerned about the frequency with which the holy water was being stolen from fonts the length and breadth of the country, ordered that all fonts should have covers. This cover was fastened down with a bar and staple and at the top of the Tickencote font is the hole which housed this simple protective device.

The medieval nave of Tickencote church had become a ruin by the late eighteenth century. It was rebuilt and various embellishments were made to the fabric in a style intended to blend with the Norman nucleus, a worthy intention. The visitor can decide how successfully it was achieved.

Places of Interest in the Neighbourhood

35. A Pigeon's Paradise (Empingham)
39. A Skirmish in the Wars of the Roses (Losecoat Field)
40. Shakespeare in the Garden (Tolethorpe Hall)

25. A FORGOTTEN CANAL WHARF

Position: Half a mile to the south-west of Market Overton.
OS Map: Grantham and surrounding area, Sheet 130.
Map Ref: SK881161.
Access: Private but easily viewed from the unclassified road which runs from Market Overton to Teigh.

The little road from Market Overton to Teigh descends steeply to the Vale of Catmose and shortly before it negotiates a sharp right-angle bend, it passes 'The Wharf'.

This small group of buildings, now converted to domestic use, has an air of faded glory. At one time it was the scene of considerable activity. It was a private wharf with a warehouse and ancillary buildings on the erstwhile Oakham Canal and was owned by one Thomas Bennett. He was a farmer who expanded his businesses to embrace malting, the provision of coal and corn and also beer-retailing. The canal would have provided him with a valuable means of transport. There were other wayside wharves on this canal including those at Saxby, Stapleford, Cottesmore and one at the canal basin at Oakham.

The Oakham Canal received parliamentary sanction in 1793 but after various difficulties, it was not until early 1803 that the first boat reached Oakham. The canal was over fifteen miles in length and at Melton Mowbray it joined the canalised River Wreake, known as the Melton Mowbray Navigation. This provided connections which allowed goods to be moved to a wide range of destinations on England's burgeoning canal system.

The Oakham Canal performed the function of many similar small rural canals in bringing coal, building materials and fertilisers, in particular, into the district and carrying away agricultural produce. Like many others, it was never a financial success. In 1844 its existence was threatened by the possibility of a railway being built from Syston, near Leicester, to Peterborough, passing through Melton Mowbray and Oakham. George Hudson, the 'Railway King', was noted for the way in which he used his considerable entrepreneurial talent to consolidate several companies into the Midland Railway, one of the largest and most progressive of the nineteenth century's railway companies. Hudson came to Oakham to smooth the way for the building of the Syston and Peterborough line, not least by offering to buy the canal and use part of its route

'The Wharf', Market Overton.

for that of the railway. One of the problems suffered by the canal was insufficient or unreliable supplies of water. Hudson arrived at a particularly propitious time because the exceptionally dry summer of 1844 had rendered the canal virtually unusable, with the result that he was able to persuade the canal's investors to sell out.

Tantalising glimpses of this relic of the optimistic 'Canal Mania' of the 1790s can be had from various by-roads north of Oakham but unfortunately access via public footpaths is not good. In some places the railway line was built over the formation of the canal, but there are a few untouched stretches of the old canal. In these, the murky waters are weed-choked, and overhanging trees and hedges encroach on the towpath, making it hard to imagine that this abandoned waterway once represented the fastest and most revolutionary form of inland transport.

Places of Interest in the Neighbourhood

2. Scene of Tom Cribb's Triumph (Thistleton)
3. A Holy Well (Ashwell)
4. Vagrancy Sign (Barrow)
13. Whipping Post and Stocks (Market Overton)
23. Collegiate Gothic (Teigh)
32. Memories of Sir Isaac Newton (Market Overton)

The old horsepond, Glaston.

26. THE FORGOTTEN HORSEPOND

Position: Glaston.
OS Map: Kettering, Corby and surrounding area, Sheet 141.
Map Ref: SK898006.
Access: The horsepond is in the village in Spring Lane, a dead end off the A47. Freely available at all times.

Ponds are common sights in old villages. In some cases all that can now be seen is a shallow, shrunken remnant of what once may have been the village's principal source of water, or its manorial fishpond. Many ponds have run dry through lack of maintenance or the lowering of water-tables as a result of drainage works and increased human consumption. Some have disappeared simply because of neglect, by being filled with rubbish or being drained and built on.

The pond at Glaston principally provided drinking water for livestock. There is a gentle slope on one bank to make access easy for wheeled vehicles. In hot weather wagons and carts would have been driven into the pond to prevent their wooden wheels drying out and shrinking, thus causing their iron tyres to become detached.

Places of Interest in the Neighbourhood
1. Mystery Maze (Wing)
12. Bishop's Palace in a Village (Lyddington)
19. A Monumental Railway Viaduct (Seaton)
29. A Fatal Epic (Uppingham)
37. Gazebo or Watch-tower? (Lyddington)
41. Burial Place of an Educational Pioneer (Uppingham)

Oakham Cemetery.

27. GOTHIC CEMETERY CHAPELS

Position: Oakham.
OS Map: Kettering, Corby and surrounding area, Sheet 141.
Map Ref: SK859096.
Access: On an unclassified road off B668 close to Oakham School playing fields. Open at all reasonable times.

Before the Burial Act for London in 1852 and its extension to the provinces in 1853, most people were buried in the churchyards of their home parishes or, where appropriate, in the cemeteries attached to nonconformist chapels. Traditional burial places had normally been able to cope with the likely number of required burials. However, the Industrial Revolution was accompanied not only by a large increase in the population but also a considerable rise in preventable and premature death.

Many town churchyards and some rural ones became overcrowded and it was not uncommon for the level of churchyards to be many feet above the church of which they were an adjunct. The lack of space was largely due to the increased use of coffins. These took up much more space than had been required for earlier burials which had largely been in winding-sheets and were the standard practice across the social classes by the eighteenth century.

Private cemeteries for those who could pay were established on the fringe of a number of big cities. In London, the pioneer was Kensal Green (1833) which was equipped with both Anglican and nonconformist chapels, a monumental entrance and catacombs served by a hydraulic lift from the chapel above.

Burial of the poor continued to be a pressing problem, acutely so when cholera and other epidemics struck. In the wake of the Act, local parishes united to establish Burial Boards which then set up and ran parochial cemeteries, to be paid for out of the Poor Rate.

The cemetery at Oakham has two chapels linked to a central porch over which stands a belfry and spirelet. The architects were Pearson Bellamy and John Spence Hardy, who designed a number of cemetery buildings. Oakham's opened in 1860, and its fame has spread because illustrations of it often appear in books on Victorian architecture.

Places of Interest in the Neighbourhood:

8. Where Butter was Sold (Oakham)
9. Birthplace of a Serial Liar (Oakham)
11. Castle with Horseshoes (Oakham)
14. The Model Railway Signal Box (Oakham)
17. Birthplace of the Rutland Dwarf (Oakham)
33. Shades of the Poor Law (Oakham)

Tinwell Smithy.

28. THE HORSESHOE DOOR

Position: Tinwell.
OS Map: Kettering, Corby and surrounding area, Sheet 141.
Map Ref: TF004064.
Access: On the A6121 in Tinwell village close to the Church. Freely visible from the road.

Tinwell is just west of Stamford, the first village in Rutland on the

A6121 towards Morcott and Uppingham. In the centre, close to the church and the pub, can be seen a huge stone horseshoe designed as part of a row of cottages. It stands about 10 feet high and was once the entrance to the village blacksmith's shop. It was built in 1848, and is of interest because the horseshoe has long been Rutland's emblem.

Designing a blacksmith's premises with a horseshoe in this way brings together two important symbols in folklore. The blacksmith worked with such mystical elements as fire and iron and also with horses and for that reason he was often credited with more knowledge of the supernatural than ordinary men. The anvil was central to his activities and it was believed to have magical qualities. Sick children used to be taken to the smithy and held over the anvil in the belief that it could help cure them. In some cases the child would be laid naked on the anvil while the blacksmith tapped the anvil lightly three times with his hammer.

Everyone knows of the good luck associated with finding a horseshoe dropped by a horse, most auspiciously if the shoe has been cast from the near hind leg of a grey mare and has seven nail holes, especially if some of the nails are still in position. Opinion varies as to whether a horseshoe above a door should have its prongs facing upwards so that the luck does not fall out or downwards so that the luck is bestowed on those passing underneath.

Places of Interest in the Neighbourhood

10. Burial place of Daniel Lambert (Stamford)
30. Gallows Inn Sign (Stamford)
34. The Tools of the Stonemason (Ketton)
38. 'Tudor' Railway Station (Stamford)
44. Health-giving waters (Stamford)
45. Gateway to Education (Stamford)
46. The Egyptian House (Stamford)
49. Brewing by Steam (Stamford)

Todd's Piece, Uppingham.

29. A FATAL EPIC

Position: Uppingham.
OS Map: Kettering, Corby and surrounding area, Sheet 141.
Map Ref: SK867997.
Access: Off A47 and A6003 just to the north of Uppingham town centre. Freely available at all times.

Legend has it that Todd was a man from Uppingham famous for his reputation as a virtuoso with the scythe. Much of his income came from winning wagers laid by people challenging him to mow a certain amount of meadowland in a specified time.

Finally he overplayed his hand. He foolishly agreed to mow a stretch of grass that could not possibly be completed in a day but his blood was up and his reputation was at stake. A large crowd turned out to watch him – some to spur him on and encourage his efforts and others with great relish fully expecting to see him fail. It was extremely hot. Todd grew weary and slowed down considerably but refused to give up. Grimly he slogged on, his admirers urging him on to one last supreme effort while his detractors scoffed at the amount still to be done.

Todd continued to address himself to his task with Herculean determination and the applause rang out around the field as he cut the last of the meadow. His bet won, Todd then keeled over like some ancient and mighty oak under the axe, crashing to the ground, stone dead.

To this day, Todd's Piece in Uppingham is a small recreation ground which recalls its namesake's courage and fortitude. Others might say that it commemorates his vanity and stubborness.

It is said that Todd's Piece once belonged to twin sisters from the nearby hamlet of Ayston, both of whom only possessed one arm. Despite their disability, they were fine spinners, buying this field in Uppingham with the proceeds of their work and then bequeathing it to the poor of the town.

Places of Interest in the Neighbourhood

1. Mystery Maze (Wing)
12. Bishop's Palace in a Village (Lyddington)
26. A Forgotten Horsepond (Glaston)
37. Gazebo or Watch-tower? (Lyddington)
41. Burial Place of an Educational Pioneer (Uppingham)

The 'gallows sign' at the George Hotel, Stamford.

30. GALLOWS INN SIGN

Position: Stamford.
OS Map: Kettering, Corby and surrounding area, Sheet 141.
Map Ref: TF030069.
Access: In St Martins (A16) close to the Town Bridge. Freely available at all times.

The 'George' at Stamford is one of the oldest and finest of Britain's ancient hostelries. One of its most striking features is its sign which straddles the street called St Martins, along which the Great North Road formerly approached Stamford from the south.

The sign at the 'George' is a rare, although by no means unique, survival of a so-called 'gallows sign'. 'Gallows signs' were both eye-catching advertisement to travellers and warnings to highwaymen of their fate if caught. In the case of the 'George' it served the additional purpose of restraining any tendency of the façade to bulge outwards.

No one is sure how old the 'George' actually is but its origins may have been with a hostelry erected by monks for pilgrims travelling to the great abbey at Crowland, about a dozen miles away to the east in the Fens. Another possibility is that the site was originally used as a hospice by the Knights of St John of Jerusalem. Much of the fabric that can be seen today was built at the end of the sixteenth century by Lord Burghley, the wily old right-hand man of Elizabeth I whose splendid mansion of Burghley House was just a mile or so away.

The 'George' exudes an atmosphere redolent of history as well it might, in view of the events it has witnessed. Charles I stayed here twice, first in 1641 and later, in 1645, around the time of his defeat at Naseby. The unpopular William III was a guest in 1696 and the Duke of Cumberland, often referred to as 'Butcher' Cumberland, resided briefly after he had massacred Bonnie Prince Charlie's forces at Culloden in 1746. Sir Walter Scott stayed at the 'George' when researching his novels or when travelling between Scotland and London.

The heyday of the 'George' was probably between about 1780 and 1850. The inn was then used by about twenty long-distance coaches daily in each direction up and down the Great North Road. Passengers had their own waiting rooms and the one on the left through the main entrance is still marked 'London' and that on the right, 'York'.

In the entrance hall of the 'George' is a painting of Daniel Lambert below which is exhibited his walking stick.

Places of Interest in the Neighbourhood

10. Burial Place of Daniel Lambert (Stamford)
31. Hunting Lodge or Dower House? (Wothorpe)
38. 'Tudor' Railway Station (Stamford)
43. Monastic Remains in a Field (Stamford)
44. Health-giving Waters (Stamford)
45. Gateway to Education (Stamford)
46. The Egyptian House (Stamford)
47. The Burghley Park Ha-Ha (Burghley Park)
48. Tudor Philanthropy (Stamford)
49. Brewing by Steam (Stamford)
50. Lodges like Bottles (Burghley)

Wothorpe Tower.

31. HUNTING LODGE OR DOWER HOUSE?

Position: Wothorpe.
OS Map: Kettering, Corby and surrounding area, Sheet 141.
Map Ref: TF024053.
Access: Off B1081. The ruins are freely visible from the bridleway to Easton-on-the-Hill. They are on farmland to which there is no public access.

Close to the A1, as its traffic thunders relentlessly north and south, and overlooking Stamford from the south-west, is the gaunt ruin of Wothorpe Tower, which is reputed to stand on the site of an ancient nunnery associated with Crowland Abbey.

This spectacular remnant of what was once a considerably larger building was built in the seventeenth century for Thomas Cecil, eldest son of William Cecil, first Lord Burghley. Legend says that it was built as somewhere to which he could escape when Burghley House itself was being spring-cleaned. Another account describes it as a hunting lodge, whilst a third suggests it was built as a dower house for the widows of successive Lord Burghleys.

Parts of Wothorpe Tower were demolished in the eighteenth century, after which the fabric was plundered of stone for use in a new stable block at Burghley House. The original building once had ogee domes like those still adorning the parent establishment at Burghley, and a courtyard flanked by two wings extending from the main building. A large, probably contemporary, barn stands close by.

Wothorpe Tower is an atmospheric, somewhat mysterious building and its potential has been recognised by film-makers who have used it, for example, when making episodes of *Dr Who*.

Places of Interest in the Neighbourhood
10. Burial Place of Daniel Lambert (Stamford)
30. Gallows Inn Sign (Stamford)
38. 'Tudor' Railway Station (Stamford)
44. Health-giving Waters (Stamford)
46. The Egyptian House (Stamford)
47. Burghley Park Ha-ha (Burghley Park)
49. Brewing by Steam (Stamford)
50. Lodges like Bottles (Burghley)

32. MEMORIES OF SIR ISAAC NEWTON

Position: Market Overton.
OS Map: Grantham and surrounding area, Sheet 130.
Map Ref: SK887164.
Access: Market Overton stands on unclassified roads off the A1 and B668. The churchyard is freely accessible at all reasonable times.

On the south-east corner of the tower of the church of St Peter and St Paul is a rather inconspicuous sundial reputed to have been given by Sir Isaac Newton (1642-1727), whose mother came from Market Overton. Newton was born into a farming family not far away at Woolsthorpe in Lincolnshire. He was a premature and sickly baby and was not expected to survive the perils of infancy. Even in adulthood, he remained puny, and it was once quipped that he could have been put into a quart mug.

Newton will forever be associated with the famous falling apple which is supposed to have caused him to question whether the force exerted by the earth in making the apple fall was the same force that helped to pull the moon in an elliptical orbit around the earth. It was the later publication of his theory of gravity and its supporting evidence that guaranteed for Newton his place as one of the greatest of all physicists.

Genius is no guarantee of other more humdrum virtues. Newton was untidy and slovenly in appearance, exceptionally absent-minded and notoriously quarrelsome, especially towards other scientists – falling out with some of the greatest names of his day. He was a vegetarian who did not marry, apparently never showing any interest in sex.

He became an MP for Cambridge University, although his only recorded utterance in the House was a request to a fellow-MP to open a window. Something even less well-known about him is that he was probably the inventor of the cat-flap. He was fond of cats and, anxious to assist them in their comings and goings, he installed a device which allowed them to do precisely that at his home at Woolsthorpe House, close to Grantham.

St Peter and St Paul is a sizeable church, part of whose tower arch is the only significant Saxon architecture in Rutland. The church was rebuilt in the fourteenth century when the settlement was at the height of its prosperity as a market town. In the area around the green, there is some sense of faded grandeur and the disposition of the streets and of the green itself, suggests that the former market place was in that vicinity.

Places of Interest in the Neighbourhood

2. Scene of Tom Cribb's Triumph (Thistleton Gap)
3. A Holy Well (Ashwell)
4. Vagrancy Sign (Barrow)
13. Whipping Post and Stocks (Market Overton)
23. Collegiate Gothic (Teigh)
25. A Forgotten Canal Wharf (Market Overton)

The sundial on the tower of Market Overton church.

33. SHADES OF THE POOR LAW

Position: Oakham.
OS Map: Kettering, Corby and surrounding area, Sheet 141.
Map Ref: SK861093.
Access: In Ashwell Road off B668 about half a mile north of Oakham town centre. The building is on private land but easily visible from Ashwell Road.

Catmose Vale Hospital in Ashwell Road, Oakham is a curious-looking building dominated by an impressive centrepiece entrance built in something of a Gothic style in 1836-7. This building provides visual evidence of an extremely unhappy period in the development of English society because it was formerly a workhouse. The issue of how to deal with poverty was a long-standing source of disagreement between the have's and have-nots but never more so than in the first half of the nineteenth century.

Economic and social change in the eighteenth century included such factors as unprecedented rates of population growth and was accompanied by a steady rise in the number of indigent people and the cost of providing them with support. At one time all schoolchildren learned about the so-called 'Speenhamland' system. This allegedly had the effect of reducing the wages of agricultural labourers because their employers knew that the parish poor law authorities would make payments from the rates that would bring the wages up to a tolerable level. The effect of this was said to have been the subsidising of low wages out of the poor rates and an escalation in the cost of providing poor relief which led eventually to the passing of the crucial Poor Law Amendment Act in 1834.

This act was exceptionally unpopular. It was designed to make substantial reductions in the financial cost of poor law provision. It did this by making the conditions and regime inside the workhouses so spartan and regimented that all but the most desperate would be deterred from applying for relief. The latter was now available, at least in theory, only to those who agreed to reside in the workhouse. The main object of those who framed this new law was to force the able-bodied unemployed who the well-to-do saw as work-shy spongers, to take work, no matter what wages and conditions were offered and thereby to cease being a burden on the poor rates.

Now it may not have been the intention to punish the impotent and helpless poor for their poverty but in practice that is what

Oakham Union Workhouse, now Catmose Vale Hospital.

happened and many of them endured near-starvation and destitution rather than apply for admission to the dreaded workhouse. Inside the workhouse husbands and wives were rigorously separated so that no 'pauper brats' would be born and children were put in their own part of the building and communication with their parents forbidden.

The Catmose Vale Hospital was originally the Oakham Union Workhouse. It is likely that its appearance was always rather less forbidding than many workhouses elsewhere but for all that its occupants would have constituted a catalogue of human misery. It is known that in 1871 it had eighty-three inmates, the oldest man being ninety-two and the oldest woman eighty-one years of age. There were several children residents, including some who were born in the workhouse. One wonders if they ever managed to escape from an institution and a system that stigmatised them for their poverty.

Places of Interest in the Neighbourhood

3. A Holy Well (Ashwell)
8. Where Butter was sold (Oakham)
9. Birthplace of a Serial Liar (Oakham)
11. Castle with Horseshoes (Oakham)
14. The Model Railway Signal Box (Oakham)
17. Birthplace of the Rutland Dwarf (Oakham)
27. Gothic Cemetery Chapels (Oakham)

A detail from a medieval illuminated manuscript.

34. THE TOOLS OF THE STONEMASON

Position: Ketton.
OS Map: Kettering, Corby and surrounding area, Sheet 141.
Map Ref: SK982043.
Access: Off the A6121 in Ketton village on unclassified road to Collyweston. The churchyard is freely accessible at all reasonable times.

Ketton is a sizeable village with many fine domestic buildings of local limestone in its ancient core. The large church is notable for its thirteenth century tower with a dominating fourteenth century broach spire which, of its kind, is fit to stand comparison with the finest in England.

Against the west wall of the churchyard is an unassuming and increasingly indecipherable headstone bearing witness to the life of

William Hibbins, a member of a long-standing family of local masons. Just visible on the headstone are a selection of the tools of Hibbins' trade.

The master mason was the most important craftsman on a medieval building site, both drafting out the initial plans and taking charge of the actual work. Beneath him were the freemasons, who did the intricate carving on high quality freestone, such as window tracery or the ribs supporting roofing vaults, the rough masons, paviors, tilers and bricklayers.

During building, the masons would erect a 'lodge', usually of timber with a thatched roof, in which to store their tools. These included hatchets, wedges, chisels, picks, hammers, sieves, buckets, mallets, trowels, gavels, compasses, squares, plumblines, shovels, hods and wheel-barrows – some of which can just about be discerned on the headstone.

At the crossroads in the village between the A6121 and the roads to Collyweston and Empingham is a handsome and well-detailed stone house which formerly belonged to the Hibbins family.

Ketton stone is a fine-grained Oolitic limestone which can be found in the Tower of London, in York Minster and Exeter Cathedral, as well as many much humbler buildings – some in the village itself. One of the pleasures to be had from Ketton stone is the way in which its appearance varies widely in different kinds of light.

Places of Interest in the Neighbourhood

28. The Horseshoe Door (Tinwell)
35. A Pigeon's Paradise (Empingham)
44. Health-giving Waters (Stamford)

35. A PIGEON'S PARADISE

Position: Empingham.
OS Map: Kettering, Corby and surrounding area, Sheet 141.
Map Ref: SK953090.
Access: On an unclassified road to Exton off the A606 north of Empingham. On private land but the dovecote may be viewed from a distance.

In a field close to the village of Empingham on the by-road to Exton stands a splendid circular stone dovecote which at one time could

The dovecote near Empingham.

have accommodated at least seven hundred nests. It is easily missed if being approached from the Empingham direction.

In medieval times, doves or pigeons provided meat and eggs for the larder, especially welcome in winter when fresh meat was almost non-existent.

Circular dovecotes had conical roofs. Internally, one or more ladders revolved around a central pivot, or potence, providing access to the rows of nesting sites that lined the walls. The mechanism that turned the potence was sometimes so well-built that no more than a touch of the finger was needed by the culverer to set it in motion. The culverer was the person in charge of the dovecote, its occupants and their eggs.

Dovecotes tended to be found close to monasteries, castles, farms and manor houses, but went out of fashion in the eighteenth century as more intensive farming methods were introduced and livestock fodder became available throughout the year.

Places of Interest in the Neighbourhood

7. The Summerhouse built as a Fort (Exton)
18. The Church in the Lake (Rutland Water)
24. A Norman Tour-de-force (Tickencote)
34. The Tools of the Stonemason (Ketton)

36. A SIMPLE COUNTRY CHURCH

Position: Brooke.
OS Map: Kettering, Corby and surrounding area, Sheet 141.
Map Ref: SK849057.
Access: The church is in the hamlet of Brooke on an unclassified minor road from Oakham to Uppingham. It is normally open during the day.
The tiny hidden-away hamlet of Brooke, two miles south-west of Oakham, takes its name from a local stream, presumably the Gwash, a word which itself is something of a curiosity. 'Gwash' may derive from an old Norse word, *waesse,* meaning a river with reeds or a river which can be waded across. The Gwash was the main stream dammed during the construction of Rutland Water.

The Elizabethan interior of St Peter, Brooke.

The church contains a number of curious items but is perhaps most notable for having been extensively restored in the Elizabethan period, about 1580, since when it has hardly been touched. It has a fine collection of Elizabethan wood furnishings including box pews, pulpit, reading desk, altar rails, screens and stalls. None are sophisticated but it is in their rustic simplicity that their charm and interest lies. There is a much older chest fashioned from a tree trunk.

The church contains work of many other periods and styles including a thirteenth century west tower, a Norman font and doorway and a recumbent alabaster effigy of 1619 of Charles Noel, of the well-known Rutland family. Carved out of woodwork in the chancel are some graffiti which probably bear witness to the intolerably lengthy sermons that were delivered in those days and the very human reaction of whiling away the time and to some extent getting one's own back by doing a little impromptu vandalism. The north door displays ancient wrought-iron hinges with some resemblance to a fish's backbone.

Another curiosity in the chancel is a gravestone which recalls the life of one Henry Rawlins who buried four wives; in 1713, 1717, 1718 and 1722 respectively. Rawlins hectic marital career finally caught up with him: he died in 1742, outlived by his fifth wife.

Close by is the site of Brooke Priory, an Augustinian establishment founded in 1153 and the only monastic foundation in Rutland. Parts of the fabric are incorporated in the house known as 'Brooke Priory' which itself is a successor to a substantial mansion built by the Noels on the priory site in the 1550s. There are some earthworks, an arch and a dovecote which are perhaps remnants of the original priory but they are on private land and not accessible.

Places of Interest in the Neighbourhood

5. A Sheela-na-gig (Braunston)
22. A Lost Village (Martinsthorpe)

37. GAZEBO OR WATCH-TOWER?

Position: Lyddington.
OS Map: Kettering, Corby and surrounding area, Sheet 141.
Map Ref: SK875970.
Access: On private property but readily visible from the main village street which is off A6003 south of Uppingham.

Lyddington is a rewarding village for those who enjoy pottering about looking at modest but attractive stone-built vernacular domestic architecture of various periods. There are numerous little lanes and alleys to explore and the gardens in the summer are a delight.

Visitors will be intrigued by the odd little building at the south-west corner of the Bede House grounds where they abut onto the main village street. Sometimes called 'The Bishop's Eye', referring to the episcopal origins of the Bede House, it is also known as the 'Garden Tower'. It is polygonal in shape with a pyramidal roof over a narrow and low passage for pedestrians. Opinion remains divided as to whether it was originally built as a watch tower or gazebo.

Nearby is the grand parish church of St Andrew which owes its size to having been a 'peculiar' – a word used to describe a church or parish exempt from the jurisdiction of the bishop in whose diocese it was situated. There is little doubt that while this sumptuous church may have been outside the Bishop of Lincoln's immediate control, it benefited from the proximity of his palace.

Inside the church, high on the chancel wall, are a number of earthenware acoustic jars. These were an early form of sound amplifier, and were positioned so as to amplify the voice of the priest during mass.

It is gratifying to know that the art of carving caricatures is not altogether lost. In 1991 the life and works of Bill Westwood, Bishop of Peterborough, were remembered with an affectionate little wall carving in which the Bishop is shown wearing his trademark spectacles. Westwood was well-known as a regular broadcaster on Radio 4's 'Thought for the Day'.

Places of Interest in the Neighbourhood
12. Bishop's Palace in a Village (Lyddington)
19. A Monumental Railway Viaduct (Seaton)
20. Did the Gunpowder Plot start here? (Stoke Dry)

'The Bishop's Eye', Lyddington.

26. A Forgotten Horsepond (Glaston)
29. A Fatal Epic (Uppingham)
41. Burial Place of an Educational Pioneer (Uppingham)

38. 'TUDOR' RAILWAY STATION

Position: Stamford.
OS Map: Kettering, Corby and surrounding area, Sheet 141.
Map Ref: TF034069.
Access: Private property but easily visible from Water Street which is off the A43 and B1443.

Close to the south bank of the River Welland where it flows parallel with Water Street in Stamford, stands what at first sight appears to be a small but architecturally stylish house of the late Tudor period. It has mullions and transoms, it bristles with finials and displays clustered chimneys galore. It is in fact the frontage of the former Stamford East Railway Station and owes its baronial style to the influence of the Cecils of Burghley House, who then owned much of the town.

The story behind one of the two small branch lines that served this station is unusual. Stamford lay athwart the Great North Road and was arguably the most important intermediate point between London and York. With the coming of the direct line of the Great Northern Railway Company from London to York in 1852 the town found itself by-passed by a route that instead went through Peterborough. It is often said that the blame for Stamford's failure to win a place on the route, and the economic doldrums that followed, lies with the 2nd Marquis of Exeter, who was concerned that the coming of a railway might further the ominous signs of radicalism among Stamford's townsfolk.

A few years later, in an attempt to make amends, the marquis put up much of the finance for a short branch railway from Stamford to a junction with the Great Northern at Essendine, belatedly providing Stamford with access to the main line. This branch line, which was at first independent, opened in 1856 and was known officially as The Stamford and Essendine Railway. Colloquially it was 'The Marquis's Railway'.

This short line, actually only just over three miles in length, led an unexceptional life until closure. Stamford East station closed in 1957 with trains being diverted into the Midland Railway's Stamford Town station, itself well worth viewing as an architectural curiosity. Even this economy could not stave of its inevitable fate and the line closed in June 1959.

For all that, the line did have its moments. On one occasion a

The former Stamford East Railway Station, now converted to modern apartments.

small tank locomotive plunged off the somewhat insubstantial bridge over the Welland and fell into the river, always thereafter being known by the ignominious and derisive nickname 'The Welland Diver'. In 1914 an engine driver approaching Stamford on a train from Essendine was apparently so carried away by the sight of a hot-air balloon passing over Stamford that he quite forgot to apply the brakes and he consequently hit the buffers at the station with considerable force.

Places of Interest in the Neighbourhood

10. Burial Place of Daniel Lambert (Stamford)
30. Gallows Inn Sign (Stamford)
31. Hunting Lodge or Dower house? (Wothorpe)
45. Gateway to Education (Stamford)
46. The Egyptian House (Stamford)
47. The Burghley House Ha-ha (Burghley Park)
48. Tudor Philanthropy (Stamford)
49. Brewing by Steam (Stamford)
50. Lodges like Bottles (Stamford)

39. A SKIRMISH IN THE WARS OF THE ROSES

Position: North-east of Empingham.
OS Map: Grantham and surrounding area, Sheet 130.
Map Ref: SK973116.
Access: Private farmland and woodland. The copse marked on the map as 'Bloody Oaks' and the open countryside are easily visible from the unclassified road to Empingham where it leaves the A1 northbound carriageway.

Edward IV was born at Rouen in 1442 and when only nineteen usurped the throne from the gentle, unworldly Henry VI. Edward was tall, athletic, strikingly handsome and exceptionally lecherous, even by the standards of royalty at that time.

Edward came to the throne during the Wars of the Roses and, because he was a Yorkist, the Lancastrians soon take up arms, gaining significant victories over the Yorkist forces at the battles of Wakefield and St Albans in 1460 and 1461, only to be routed by Edward at the Battle of Towton in Yorkshire, also in 1461.

Edward's marriage, at first kept secret, to Elizabeth Woodville, managed to alienate his leading supporter, the immensely powerful Earl of Warwick who left in a huff to join the Lancastrians and then spent several years attempting to launch an uprising against Edward. In 1470, Warwick's machinations led to rebellions in Wales and Lincolnshire. The latter was led by Sir Robert Welles. The king moved swiftly and decisively, marching to Stamford and seizing Lord Welles who was Sir Robert's father and Sir Thomas Dymock and having them executed.

In March 1470 Edward marched out of Stamford against the rebels. In a field near Empingham and close to the present A1 a most extraordinary 'battle' then took place. The king's forces launched an artillery bombardment which so terrified the rebels that many scattered and ran away, removing their coats bearing the tell-tale Welles arms as they did so. Welles himself was captured and executed.

This ignominious defeat for the Lancastrians, with a minimum actual passage of arms, has been dubbed, ironically, as 'The Battle of Losecoat Field'. Fighting probably took place not only at 'Bloody Oaks' but in the nearby village of Pickworth where many buildings were ransacked and demolished. A mass grave was unearthed in the

A contemporary depiction of a skirmish during the Wars of the Roses.

1970s which contained the remains of large numbers of men who appeared to have been slaughtered at the same time.

Places of Interest in the Neighbourhood

7. The Summerhouse built as a Fort (Exton)
15. 'Ram Jam Inn' (Stretton)
16. 'Jackson-Stops' Pub Sign (Stretton)
21. A Mason's Book of Samples (Greetham)
24. A Norman Tour-de-force (Tickencote)
35. A Pigeon's Paradise (Empingham)

Tolethorpe Hall.

40. SHAKESPEARE IN THE GARDEN

Position: Tolethorpe.
OS Map: Grantham and surrounding district, Sheet 130.
Map Ref: TF024102.
Access: Private grounds but open to the public during the Shakespeare season. On an unclassified road off A121 to the west of Ryhall.

The Stamford Shakespeare Company was formed in 1968 and at first put on its productions in the Monastery Garden of the 'George Hotel' in Stamford. In 1976, in need of a new venue, they managed to buy Tolethorpe Hall, then in a terrible state of repair. Today the Rutland Open Air Theatre has gained an enviable reputation for the high quality not only of the acting but also of the costumes, props and settings. So on warm summer evenings the public are treated to performances in what is almost an open-air theatre, the auditorium being under a permanent awning although the stage is open to the elements.

Tolethorpe Hall is close to the village of Little Casterton and was originally a medieval manor house which came into the hands of the Browne family. It was rebuilt in the late sixteenth century, enlarged in the seventeenth century and restored and partly rebuilt in the 1860s. Tolethorpe was famous in earlier years for being the birthplace of a turbulent priest. Here was born Robert Browne, (1550-1603), who is often regarded as the founder of the principle of congregationalism in the Christian Church, that is, the idea that the layfolk should be able to gather for worship without an ordained priest and outside the aegis of the established church. He broke with the Church of England in 1581.

Places of Interest in the Neighbourhood
42. 'The Hurdler' Pub Sign (Stamford)
43. Monastic Remains in a Field (Stamford)
45. Gateway to Education (Stamford)
46. The Egyptian House (Stamford)
48. Tudor Philanthropy (Stamford)
49. Brewing by Steam (Stamford)

The monument to Edward Thring.

41. BURIAL PLACE OF AN EDUCATIONAL PIONEER

Position: Uppingham.
OS Map: Kettering, Corby and surrounding area, Sheet 141.
Map Ref: SK866998.
Access: At the southern end of the churchyard off the Market Place. Freely accessible at all reasonable times.

One of the most illustrious of the many worthies buried in the churchyard of St Peter and St Paul, in the centre of the small town of Uppingham, is Edward Thring, (1821-1887). His place of interment is marked by a substantial cross.

Thring was born in Somerset and educated at Eton and King's College, Cambridge. He was ordained in 1846. In 1853 he became headmaster of what was then Uppingham Grammar School. The school had been founded in 1584 by Robert Johnson who established Oakham School at the same time. Uppingham Grammar School, like many other ancient educational establishments in the nineteenth century, had fallen on hard times. Crucially, it lacked sufficient pupils and therefore adequate income to be viable. When he took over, the school had forty-five boys, of whom about half were boarders allowed to run wild. The tiny classroom, in which teaching had taken place before Thring's time, can still be seen in the churchyard.

Thring turned the school round so that within ten years it had three hundred pupils and had become a model for the fee-paying 'public' schools to which the Victorian well-to-do classes sent their boys. They did so in order for them to gain a modicum of education, mostly in the Classics. More importantly they also looked to these schools to inculcate in the boys a set of shared values and the sense of being chosen to administer Britain and its Empire.

Thring's influence extended way beyond Uppingham. He wrote extensively on education, was one of the founders of the Headmaster's Conference of Britain's top schools and was before his time in emphasising the need for improved educational opportunities for girls.

Places of Interest in the Neighbourhood

12. Bishop's Palace in a Village (Lyddington)
20. Did the Gunpowder Plot start here? (Stoke Dry)
26. A Forgotten Horsepond (Glaston)
29. A Fatal Epic (Uppingham)
37. Gazebo or Watch-tower? (Lyddington)

42. 'THE HURDLER' PUB SIGN

Position: Stamford.
OS Map: Kettering, Corby and surrounding area, Sheet 141.
Map Ref: TF031077.
Access: New Cross Street off A6121 near the Recreation Ground north of Stamford town centre. Freely accessible at all times.

Close to the centre of Stamford is an unassuming 1930s pub with a unique name. This commemorates the achievements of the 6th Marquis of Exeter who, when known as David Cecil, then Lord Burghley, gained international fame as an athlete. He won a gold medal in the four hundred metres hurdles at the 1928 Olympics.

While he was an undergraduate at Trinity College, Cambridge in 1927, he gained the coveted prize known as 'victory over the clock'. This involved sprinting around the four sides of the Great Court of Trinity College while the clock was striking twelve – which he did, albeit by the skin of his teeth. In the film 'Chariots of Fire', Burghley was played by Nigel Havers, but sadly the film showed another competitor, Harold Abrahams, winning this race against the clock. When he saw the film, the marquis was deeply offended by this misrepresentation of historic fact.

Burghley was popular everywhere he went, not only because of his athletic prowess but for his complete lack of pomposity or aristocratic hauteur. Another of his feats was sprinting round the promenade deck of the *Queen Mary.* He did this in fifty-eight seconds while dressed in formal evening wear, which must have been no mean achievement. In many ways he was one of the very last of Britain's eccentric sporting squires or aristocrats

After retiring from active sport, he gained an enviable reputation for the work he did to enhance the ethos of amateurism in athletics. He was, for example, President of the International Amateur Athletics Federation, Chairman of the British Olympic Association and a member of the International Olympic Committee. There is little doubt that his influence was behind the decision to locate the 1948 Olympic Games in England.

Places of Interest in the Neighbourhood
10. Burial Place of Daniel Lambert (Stamford)
30. Gallows Inn Sign (Stamford)
38. 'Tudor' Railway Station (Stamford)

'The Hurdler', Stamford.

43. Monastic Remains in a Field (Stamford)
45. Gateway to Education (Stamford)
46. The Egyptian House (Stamford)
48. Tudor Philanthropy (Stamford)
49. Brewing by Steam (Stamford)

43. MONASTIC REMAINS IN A FIELD

Position: Stamford.
OS Map: Kettering, Corby and surrounding area, Sheet 141.
Map Ref: TF037073.
Access: Off the A16 east of Stamford town centre. On private land and can be viewed from the road or approached through a gate into the adjoining field.

What can be seen today is only a remnant of the west front, the nave and part of the north arcade of the conventual church of a small priory dedicated to St Leonard and founded in 1082. Although only a fragment it is still impressive. The priory would at one time have been a considerably larger accumulation of buildings and archaeological excavations have shown that a cloister existed to the south and there was at least one transept and a choir. It was a Benedictine establishment under the tutelage of Durham Abbey, acting effectively as a base from which its various business interests in this part of the country could be administered.

Stamford as benefited a town of its importance had a large number of churches in medieval times, of which five are still in use. It also possessed three monastic establishments; St Leonard's, St Mary and St Michael (Benedictines) and Newstead Priory (Austin Canons). All four of the mendicant orders of friars were represented in Stamford. They were the Dominicans (Blackfriars), Franciscans (Greyfriars), Carmelites (Whitefriars) and Austin Friars. Like the monastic establishments, they were suppressed in the 1530s.

Places of Interest in the Neighbourhood
10. Burial Place of Daniel Lambert (Stamford)
30. Gallows Inn Sign (Stamford)
38. 'Tudor' Railway Station (Stamford)
42. 'The Hurdler' Pub Sign (Stamford)
45. Gateway to Education (Stamford)
46. The Egyptian House (Stamford)
48. Tudor Philanthropy (Stamford)
49. Brewing with Steam (Stamford)

The remains of St Leonard's Priory, Stamford.

44. HEALTH-GIVING WATERS

Position: Stamford.
OS Map: Kettering, Corby and surrounding area, Sheet 141.
Map Ref: TL019060.
Access: There is no vehicular access to the site of the spring but a clearly defined footpath runs from Stamford through the Meadows and along the banks of the Welland past the Spa to Tinwell.

In 1790 Horace Walpole, the well-known bon vivant and man of letters, is purported to have said, 'One would think the English were ducks; they are for ever waddling to the waters.' He was referring to the extraordinary popularity at that time among the rich for visiting inland watering places, ostensibly to take the therapeutic mineral-rich waters, but more often because they played a minor part in the social calendar.

By imbibing or bathing in the waters, those who patronised such places as Cheltenham, Tunbridge Wells and Bath hoped to treat ailments which were as likely to be imagined as real, and often stemmed from simple over-indulgence. They spent freely and the successful spa towns attracted doctors, quacks, mountebanks, confidence-tricksters, those seeking matrimony and a multitude of

The well-head to Stamford 'spa'.

other hangers-on.

Across the country, speculators were keen to find sources of mineral water which could then be tapped and exploited by additionally providing a pump room, changing rooms and one or two doctors on hand to advise on the necessary therapeutic regimen. Assembly rooms, winter gardens, hotels and other facilities might follow if the place caught on.

Fashion was capricious, and Stamford's hopes of becoming a flourishing spa were never realised. What can be seen today is a curious conical stone well-head and nearby a plaque with the following inscription:

THE STAMFORD SPA

The Mineral (Ironstone) spring was brought into use in 1819 and much sought after by persons affected by various ailments in the belief that this water had medicinal properties. The stone head was placed here by order of John Paradise in 1864.

The water at 52° F had a specific gravity of 1.0015 and two pints contained 10.68 grains of solid matter.

Oxide of Iron 0.08; Carbonate of Lime 4.8; Muriot of Soda 1.0; Sulphate of Lime 4.4;
Silex 0.4.

Places of Interest in the Neighbourhood

10. Burial Place of Daniel Lambert (Stamford)
28. Horseshoe Door to Former Smithy (Tinwell)
30. Gallows Inn Sign (Stamford)
38. 'Tudor' Railway Station (Stamford)
46. The Egyptian House (Stamford)
49. Brewing with Steam (Stamford)

45. GATEWAY TO EDUCATION

Position: Stamford.
OS Map: Kettering, Corby and surrounding area, Sheet 141.
Map Ref: TF033074.
Access: In St Paul's Street, a few hundred yards east of Stamford town centre. Freely accessible at all times.

On the south side of St Paul's Street stands an inconspicuous doorway under an arch in a stone wall. It dates from the thirteenth century and is generally reckoned to mark the entrance to the site of Brazenose Hall in which a group of masters and students made a

Brazenose Gate.

break from Oxford University and attempted to set up a rival establishment in Stamford.

Historically, there is no doubt that there was a secession from Oxford in 1333 and that a group of disillusioned masters and learners moved first to Northampton and then to Stamford. It seems that the move was not a success and that some of them had already returned to Oxford before 1335. For all that, the authorities at both Oxford and Cambridge viewed this development with grave concern and moves were made to force students at Oxford to utter an oath that they would have nothing academically to do with Stamford. The services of the King were required to force the hardline dissidents to leave the town. The oath concerning Stamford continued to be taken by all new undergraduates at Oxford until 1854!

The rather fine door knocker to be seen today is unfortunately not the original. This can be found adorning Brazenose College in Oxford whence it was taken from Stamford in 1890 under the apprehension that it had earlier been removed from Oxford.

In the light of this farrago of confusion, it is interesting to note that, after the Second World War, Stamford was considered as the site for a university to act as an overspill to Oxford and Cambridge. Later it was mentioned as the possible site for one of the new wave of universities founded in the 1960s, such as Warwick, East Anglia and York. Nothing came of these ideas.

Places of Interest in the Neighbourhood

10. Burial Place of Daniel Lambert (Stamford)
30. Gallows Inn Sign (Stamford)
38. 'Tudor' Railway Station (Stamford)
42. 'The Hurdler' Pub Sign (Stamford)
43. Monastic Remains in a Field (Stamford)
46. The Egyptian House (Stamford)
48. Tudor Philanthropy (Stamford)
49. Brewing with Steam (Stamford)

46. THE EGYPTIAN HOUSE

Position: Stamford.
OS Map: Kettering, Corby and surrounding area, Sheet 141.
Map Ref: TF026070.
Access: Opposite the bus station on St Peter's Street in the town centre. A private building currently in use as a language school. The frontage may be freely viewed at any time.

The Stamford Institution used to be housed in this rather odd-looking building in St Peter's Street. The building was designed by Bryan Browning, architect of Oakham workhouse, probably in 1842.

The Institution was built at a time when Stamford's considerable prosperity was about to be threatened by the building of a main line railway from London to York, reducing traffic on the Great North Road and badly affecting the town's economy. All this lay in the future in 1842 and the Institute's backers went confidently ahead with the building, fitting out and opening what was intended to be the centre for the town's intelligentsia and literati. It incorporated a museum, library, lecture hall and laboratory and even had a camera obscura on the roof although this was removed in 1910.

Stylistically, the Stamford Institution can best be described as Greek Revival with Egyptian motifs, for which there was then a short-lived fashion. This was perhaps the result of a surge of interest in Egyptian antiquities and culture after Nelson's decisive victory over the French at the Battle of the Nile.

Other buildings in this decidedly quirky pseudo-Egyptian genre include the rather better-known Temple Mills at Leeds, the exceptionally flamboyant 'Egyptian House' in Penzance and the remarkable, but less often mentioned or viewed, Freemasons' Temple at Boston.

Places of Interest in the Neighbourhood
10. Burial Place of Daniel Lambert (Stamford)
30. Gallows Inn-Sign (Stamford)
38. 'Tudor' Railway Station (Stamford)
44. Health-giving waters (Stamford)
45. Gateway to Education (Stamford)
48. Tudor Philanthropy (Stamford)
49. Brewing with Steam (Stamford)

Stamford Institution.

47. THE BURGHLEY HOUSE HA-HA

Position: Stamford.
OS Map: Kettering, Corby and surrounding area, Sheet 141.
Map Ref: TF046062.
Access: In Burghley Park, close to Burghley House. The Park is normally freely open to pedestrians.

St Martins-Without or Stamford Baron is the name given to that part of Stamford which lies on the south side of the River Welland and is therefore outside Lincolnshire. It contains Burghley Park, seven miles in circumference, in which stands the magnificent Elizabethan mansion of Burghley House. This provides a wonderful visual reminder of the political success of that great Elizabethan statesman, William Cecil (1520-1598).

In 1558 Elizabeth appointed him her chief secretary of state and for forty years he had a crucial influence on England's domestic and foreign policies. In 1571 he was created Baron Burghley and in 1572 his continuing usefulness to the queen was further rewarded when he was made Lord High Treasurer, an office he held until his death, only a few years before the queen herself died.

The house stands where there was once an ancient monastic cell and later a manor house. Fragments of these were incorporated in this mansion which appears to have been built between 1550 and 1587, possibly to the design of John Thorpe, the master builder of his day. It is an awe-inspiring sight with its numerous cupolas, pinnacles and chimneys and it contains no less than 145 rooms, built around a central courtyard.

The estate surrounding Burghley House was transformed in the latest picturesque fashion by none other than Lancelot 'Capability' Brown. He reputedly gained this curious nickname because when asked whether he would take on a commission and how he would tackle it, he would reply enthusiastically, 'There is a capability, Sir, there is a capability.' He carried out work at Burghley over a lengthy period, from 1756 to 1779, and his work included the conversion of streams into a lake, the building of a bath house, a conservatory and orangery, plantations and the handsome Lion Bridge over the new lake, not far from the ha-ha. His work at Burghley seems to have given Brown particular satisfaction.

Dating from this time is the ha-ha which acts as a boundary to the lawns on the north-western frontage of the house. A ha-ha is

The ha-ha, Burghley House.

probably the best-known form of visual trickery used in landscape design. It consists of a ditch surrounding a garden, a lawn or a churchyard and is designed to create a barrier keeping livestock out while deceiving the eye by making it appear that the surrounding park and the enclosed land are continuous.

Places of Interest in the Neighbourhood

10. Burial Place of Daniel Lambert (Stamford)
30. Gallows Inn Sign (Stamford)
31. Hunting Lodge or Dower House? (Wothorpe)
38. 'Tudor' Railway Station (Stamford)
50. Lodges like Bottles (Burghley Park)

48. TUDOR PHILANTHROPY

Position: Stamford.
OS Map: Kettering, Corby and surrounding area, Sheet 141.
Map Ref: TF030073.
Access: On the north side of Broad Street in Stamford town centre. There are occasional open days in the summer but the exterior can be freely viewed at any time.

In Browne's Hospital in Broad Street, Stamford possesses one of the finest surviving medieval almshouses in the United Kingdom.

Establishments of this sort were set up as charitable concerns to care for the elderly, the infirm, the poor and for wayfarers such as pilgrims. They were frequently similar in plan to monastic infirmaries, having a chapel, an infirmary hall and accommodation, often in the form of a dormitory or in small apartments. Each almshouse was supervised by a warden or master.

In Tudor times they lost any remaining religious function and in common with institutions set up later became residences which cared for those who could not look after themselves, often selecting their inmates after careful and lengthy enquiries as to their probity and rectitude.

Browne's Hospital was founded to accomodate 10 to 12 poor men in the 1480s by William Browne, a local man who had become wealthy trading in wool. He is depicted with his wife on a commemorative brass of 1489 in All Saints Parish Church, close by, with two woolpacks at his feet.

Places of Interest in the Neighbourhood

10. Burial Place of Daniel Lambert (Stamford)
30. Gallows Inn Sign (Stamford)
38. 'Tudor' Railway Station (Stamford)
42. 'The Hurdler' Pub Sign (Stamford)
43. Monastic Remains in a Field (Stamford)
45. Gateway to Education (Stamford)
46. The Egyptian House (Stamford)
49. Brewing by Steam (Stamford)

Browne's Hospital, Stamford.

49. BREWING BY STEAM

Position: Stamford.
OS Map: Kettering, Corby and surrounding area, Sheet 141.
Map Ref: TF028071.
Access: Visible at all times from St Peter's Street or All Saints Square. There are brewery visits.

At the junction of St Peter's Street and Scotgate in the centre of Stamford is a well-preserved small brewery of the sort that most towns possessed until the consolidation, mergers, takeovers and closures which were characteristic of the brewing industry in the twentieth century.

Ale and beer are ancient beverages. Ale, dark, sweet and often flavoured with herbs was being brewed in Britain long before beer arrived on the scene. The latter was lighter in colour and contained hops which were useful both for giving beer a bitter flavour and, with their essential oils, helping to prolong its life. Beer was introduced to this country in late medieval times by immigrants from the Low Countries and it took a considerable time before it was commonly accepted. The words 'ale' and 'beer' refer strictly to different beverages but are now used interchangeably.

The other raw materials for brewing consist of water, sugar, barley and yeast. It was the differing combinations of these ingredients and the presence in the water of various minerals which gave distinctiveness to what were in the past genuine 'local brews'. This meant that there were significant differences in the flavour and character of beers brewed in Stamford from those, for example, brewed in Nottingham.

Water is needed in many parts of the brewing process. The requirements of the brewing industry acted as a significant demand factor stimulating the development of steam engines in the eighteenth and nineteenth centuries. Steam power was harnessed to assist the movement of the ingredients around breweries, many of which, like All Saints Brewery, were built on a tower principle. Having used steam to raise the ingredients, gravity then moved them, especially the water or 'liquor' as brewers call it, around the building for such processes as mashing, boiling, fermentation and storing.

Brewing commenced on the All Saints site in 1825 and the brewery was purchased by Melbourn Brothers in 1869. They proceeded to build up a small estate of tied houses which stood at

All Saints Brewery, Stamford.

thirty-two when brewing ceased in 1974.

All Saints Brewery is a working museum of brewing which produces fruit and other specialist beers and still contains much early brewing equipment including a mash tun, copper, fermenting vessels and the original steam engine.

Other defunct common brewers in Stamford were Phillips Stamford Brewery in Water Street; Lowe, Son and Cobbold of 6 & 7 Broad Street and G & H.R. Hunt also of Water Street. The name of the latter can still easily be seen carved on the frontage of part of the old brewery buildings, overlooking the River Welland.

Places of Interest in the Neighbourhood

10. Burial Place of Daniel Lambert (Stamford)
30. Gallows Inn Sign (Stamford)
38. 'Tudor' Railway Station (Stamford)
42. 'The Hurdler' Pub Sign (Stamford)
43. Monastic Remains in a Field (Stamford)
44. Health-giving Waters (Stamford)
45. Gateway to Education (Stamford)
46. The Egyptian House (Stamford)
48. Tudor Philanthropy (Stamford)

50. LODGES LIKE BOTTLES

Position: Stamford.
OS Map: Kettering, Corby and surrounding area, Sheet 141.
Map Ref: TF033062.
Access: On the east side of the B1081 about a mile out of Stamford. Freely visible from the road at all times. There is no regular vehicular access into or out of these gates for the general public. Pedestrians can pass through when Burghley Park is open.

William Legg was a local architect who put his own very individual stamp on a number of buildings in the Stamford area, including Fort Henry on the Exton Park Estate (No 7). His handiwork can still be seen in Stamford's High Street where he designed a rather grand Tuscan frontage or portico for what at that time was the local shambles or butchers' market. This was opened in 1808 and about a century later the building was converted into a library and museum. It is still the town's library. It is generally considered that Legg took his inspiration for this grandiloquent shambles from the church of St Paul's in Covent Garden, London, designed by Inigo Jones.

The inspiration for the lodges that Legg designed for the western entrance to Burghley Park is less obvious. These are on the Old North Road as it climbs southwards out of Stamford and were built in 1801. The style has been described somewhat kindly as 'Jacobethan' and clearly owes something to the nearby presence of Wothorpe Tower and Burghley House itself. Their familiar name as the 'Bottle Lodges' seems very appropriate. They are eye-catching curiosities and an excellent foil for the architectural grandeur of Burghley House.

Places of Interest in the Neighbourhood
10. Burial Place of Daniel Lambert (Stamford)
30. Gallows Inn Sign (Stamford)
31. Hunting Lodge or Dower House? (Wothorpe)
38. 'Tudor' Railway Station (Stamford)
46. The Egyptian House (Stamford)
47. The Burghley House Ha-ha (Burghley)
49. Brewing with Steam (Stamford)

The western entrance to Burghley Park.

Index

Places by page number

Ashwell 14
Barrow 16
Braunston-in-Rutland 18
Brooke 78
Burghley 100
Clipsham 20
Empingham 76, 84
Exton 21
Glaston 60
Greetham 50
Ketton 74
Losecoat Field 84
Lyddington 32, 80
Market Overton 34, 58, 70
Martinsthorpe 52
Normanton 44
Oakham 23, 25, 30, 36, 42
Seaton 46
Stamford 27, 67, 82, 90, 92, 94, 96, 98, 100, 102, 104, 106
Stoke Dry 48
Stretton 38, 40
Teigh 54
Thistleton Gap 12
Tickencote 56
Tinwell 63
Tolethorpe 86
Uppingham 65, 88
Wing 10
Wothorpe 69